WORDS
BECOME
YOU

Order this book online at www.trafford.com/07-2963
or email orders@trafford.com

Most Trafford titles are also available at major online book retailers.

© Copyright 2008 Gareth Sirotnik.

Book Design by Ben Ze Wang.

Note for Librarians: A cataloguing record for this book is available from Library
and Archives Canada at www.collectionscanada.ca/amicus/index-e.html

Printed in Victoria, BC, Canada.

ISBN: 978-1-4251-6431-7

We at Trafford believe that it is the responsibility of us all, as both individuals
and corporations, to make choices that are environmentally and socially sound.
You, in turn, are supporting this responsible conduct each time you purchase a
Trafford book, or make use of our publishing services. To find out how you are
helping, please visit www.trafford.com/responsiblepublishing.html

Our mission is to efficiently provide the world's finest, most comprehensive
book publishing service, enabling every author to experience success.
To find out how to publish your book, your way, and have it available
worldwide, visit us online at www.trafford.com/10510

Trafford
PUBLISHING™

www.trafford.com

North America & international
toll-free: 1 888 232 4444 (USA & Canada)
phone: 250 383 6864 ♦ fax: 250 383 6804
email: info@trafford.com

The United Kingdom & Europe
phone: +44 (0)1865 722 113 ♦ local rate: 0845 230 9601
facsimile: +44 (0)1865 722 868 ♦ email: info.uk@trafford.com

10 9 8 7 6 5 4 3 2 1

WORDS
BECOME
YOU

Communicating (and Living) More Fluently

A GUIDE FOR EVERYONE

Gareth Sirotnik

So well thy words become thee as thy wounds: They smack of honour both.

King Duncan replying to a loyal, wounded captain
– William Shakespeare, *The Tragedy of Macbeth*

Contents

Communication, Your Birthright

You already possess all the powers you need to communicate and live in all respects more easily and instinctively – more fluently. The ten powers described in this book merely help you to liberate your natural inborn talents. Connect with others, express yourself genuinely, and words become you.

COMMUNICATION IS YOUR BIRTHRIGHT. You are born into this world possessing all the powers you need to connect to your fellow beings and the world around you. You do not have to get in touch: you already are. You're prewired for communication.

We each come into life fully experiencing, inseparably from ourselves, everyone and everything in every moment. As infants, we're automatically connected to our world, even without language. A baby does not separate self from other. Watch how an infant stares at the shiny toys hanging from above its crib. See how the child and mother gaze at one another. No separation! This connection is the purest form of communication – immediate, total, direct. Communication is life itself.

Unfortunately, this natural connection blurs over time. Growing up and learning to see ourselves separate from everything else, we lose contact with our innate faculties. To reawaken these powers of communication we can use a little help. That's what you'll find in the following pages: guidance on how to release pent-up abilities for communicating – writing in particular – and living life in all respects more easily and instinctively: that's *fluency*.

Whatever your occupation or role in life, the ten tools described in this book will help you to communicate with less effort and greater confidence. Since fewer and fewer people seem able to do so – especially through writing – communicating articulately gives you extra leverage in whatever you set out to accomplish at work, in groups, and with family and friends.

Writing articulately gives you extra leverage.

We all experience failures in communicating: failures in confidence and in living more deeply connected to the people and world around us. These so-called failures are actually opportunities for learning and growth. Here's just one example of failure drawn from many in my own life experience.

MY STORY

Communication breakdown

When Quality Circles and similar methods for building employee participation became a fad in the 1980s, a multinational paper products company decided to introduce a trial program at one of their North American plants. Companies were jumping on the bandwagon hoping to emulate the success Japanese industries had in garnering employee commitment to quality production.

The paper products company sought the advice of a large New York–based international management consulting firm. The lead consultant recommended the company initiate the process by seeking their employees' input into what kind of program they themselves thought would work. It made sense that if they wanted to involve people they should begin by involving them from the start.

I inherited the project when I joined the firm as the communication specialist in one of their branch offices. They headhunted me when the position became vacant. Although I returned to my freelance practice after a year, I gained new insight into the workings of the consulting industry.

This particular firm specialized in pension and benefits plans, and internal corporate communication. The firm's fortunes seemed immune to economic ups and downs. When the economy boomed, clients needed help organizing benefits for new employees; when things turned sour, they sought guidance processing discharged workers. Either way, up or down, the consulting firm prospered.

Soon after joining the firm, I tabulated and analyzed the results of a written survey that had been circulated to all employees at the plant where the company intended to introduce the new program. Next, over a period of several weeks, I conducted a series of focus groups with employees.

The results were clear. As I explained to the company's executive committee when I met with them to report my findings, a remarkably high percentage of their employees felt that no involvement program of any kind would work. In their view, the corporate culture was so paternalistic that the company's leadership would be unreceptive to criticism.

The moment I reported my conclusion, the CEO thumped the desk with his fist and shouted,

"How dare you tell us that? How dare you?" I watched in silence, stunned at first, then hiding my amusement and self-satisfaction.

Whenever I tell this story people laugh, as I did, at the transparency of the CEO's reaction: how, in his very response to the report's findings, he and the other executives, who concurred in his outrage, substantiated the skepticism their employees had voiced. This was not a company open to criticism and collaborative communication.

As I came to realize later, however, the real communication breakdown in this instance was not that of the executive committee, but mine. I was the one who had not listened effectively – that is, not *heard* clearly what was said to me. Having learned what I did from the survey and focus groups about how employees perceived the company's leadership style, I should have proceeded accordingly.

Alerted to the executives' paternalistic mindset, I could have communicated the findings more sensitively, gradually building up the picture rather than hitting them over the head with the conclusion so dramatically at the start. Instead of alienating them, I could have helped the executives to accept the results despite their predisposition, learn from the conclusions, and perhaps even change their attitudes at least enough to initiate the process of involving their employees.

In other words, I should have communicated in a fashion informed by the nature of my audience, the executives. Instead, I acted out of self-satisfied pride at having uncovered some "deep truth" about the company. But my job was to help the client evolve, not to act out like a smart aleck. Clearly I, too, needed to evolve.

Looking at writing – and life in general

The ten powers presented in this book apply to life and communication in general but focus on writing. People often feel anxious when faced with a writing task. I certainly have, even in writing these very words. In fact, I've rewritten them a number of times, trying to get my meaning just right, anxious to prove myself to others, fearful of failure. That's the little dialogue going on inside my head.

Connecting with other people and engaging in life more fully come easily – if you unleash your innate faculties.

Let's admit it, communication is stressful. Filling a blank page (or computer screen), stepping up to the podium, engaging in group discussion, approaching an awkward topic with a friend – it makes us uncomfortable. Which is odd, since communication, as I said at the beginning, is our natural state of being. Communication brings us together with who we are, what we do, and the world we're part of. But much of the time we don't feel or act connected. As a result, communication becomes awkward, deceitful, misunderstood, or avoided.

It doesn't have to be this way. Connecting with other people and engaging in life more fully come easily – if you unleash your innate faculties.

I discovered and honed my own communication skills while working as a professional writer and consultant. For more than thirty years I've helped many individuals, companies, and organizations with their communication strategies and programs. I've written numerous articles, brochures, presentations, and ads, and created many successful brands.

But the insights and practical tips set out in the following pages apply to everyone, regardless of your profession or experience. They also apply to all types of communication, from marketing, reports, websites, and visual media to creative writing, public speaking, personal letters, and everyday conversation.

Communication brings us together with who we are, what we do, and the world we're part of.

While seen through the window of writing, however, the powers described in this book point to something deeper: how to live a more satisfying life by expressing yourself genuinely and relating fully to the world and people around you. In the process of writing the book, while examining my own experience, I realized that my insights about writing and communication apply to life more broadly. And when it comes to living, we are each our own resident expert. We need only tap more deeply into our inborn talents.

Communication issues relate to all aspects of life.

Here, then, in summary are the ten powers set out in the following pages.

The book begins with a look at "nothing": the intimidating blank mind, blank page, or blank screen we first encounter when we put pen to paper or fingers to keys, or when we confront any challenging life situation, and hit a void. Not knowing how to proceed arouses feelings of insecurity, even terror for some. But this "nothing" or emptiness, as chapter one explains, actually provides you with a great reservoir of natural *insight* – if you develop the confidence to use it.

Chapter two continues in this vein, describing how to release your inherent ability for acquiring knowledge through *perception:* by opening your senses – hearing, in particular – and realizing things just as they are. In doing so, anything is knowable and anything can be communicated.

The book next looks at exploiting your *intuition.* Gut reactions help you to preempt problems and uncover crucial clues for carrying out any project or achieving any aim.

Chapters four to seven examine the practical, hands-on process of writing and communicating: employing the power of *synthesis* to turn your ideas into singular coherent messages; drawing on your *creativity* to respond to ever-changing conditions; establishing *clarity* in what seems like a chaotic mass of endless detail; and exercising *articulation* to convey your central message and interest your audience from the start.

The next two chapters highlight your underlying strengths for effective communication – and better living in general. The more you speak, write, and act with personal *conviction,* the book explains, the more meaningfully you connect with people. Through your power of *empathy,* you deepen your communication by realizing how others hear your words and interpret what you say.

All of these abilities are aspects of one essential power – self-*confidence.* The book's final chapter looks at confidence, however, not in the self that feels isolated and separate but in the deeper, more complete self that's interconnected and interdependent with the world.

Early in each chapter I tell a story drawn from my own experience. At the end of the chapter you'll find a brief writing exercise which, when completed, you can submit to the book's website www.WordsBecomeYou.com.

Hearing more than me

Before proceeding, consider first why virtually all of us run into so many problems with communication, whether written, spoken, electronic, visualized, or expressed through gestures and body language. If it's so natural, why does human connection so readily break down?

In short, because instead of genuinely relating to the people we're interacting with, we tend to get wrapped up in ourselves – in too much *me*. When we communicate, often we're actually listening to ourselves, and not only when we're talking but also when we're supposedly listening. Through long habit, without our realizing it, our internal dialogues, anxieties, and prejudices drown out and disrupt the human exchanges we engage in. Communication fails because all too often we're only hearing ourselves.

Internal dialogues disrupt human exchange.

Self-absorption isn't just a problem between individual people. Obsession with identity causes communication to break down between whole groups and communities, and among nations. Marriages collapse over it. Businesses fail because of it. Countries go to war over it.

In families and between couples and friends, little misunderstandings frequently grow into grudges that poison relationships and last a lifetime. Between nations and ethnic groups, communication breakdowns cause wounds and hatreds that are passed down from generation to generation, locking people into tragic habits of fear and loathing and generating endless cycles of wrath and brutality. Feuds, intimidation, bullying, withdrawal, confrontation, war, genocide: over and over again, throughout human history, the cycle repeats itself.

It's not as if communication breakdowns go unrecognized. After elaborate and expensive organizational studies, business and other leaders inevitably seem to conclude, "Communication is our greatest problem." I've heard these exact words spoken again and again by my clients and acquaintances, and seen them in numerous reports and articles.

Communication fails because all too often we're only hearing ourselves.

Yet few individuals, families, or organizations do anything fundamental to alter the situation. Other, seemingly more urgent, day-to-day priorities take away the focus and energy from solving underlying issues. Communication shortcomings fester away, gradually infecting the environment at deeper and deeper levels until the problems become endemic and part of the culture itself.

People don't genuinely speak to or hear each other when they've grown accustomed to holding back or ignoring what's happening, hearing only themselves. In fact, people often fear that openness makes them vulnerable. So nobody says anything – well, not the truth anyway. Organizations are rife with rumors and gossip; but that's not genuine communication, just as spying and subversion do not substitute for genuine diplomacy and healthy international relations.

I'm not suggesting that communication alone will solve all problems among people and nations. People have always competed and fought over energy, food, water, land, and other resources. If you look at history or recent events, battles fought over principle or ideology often mask issues of resource control. But in a deeper sense, communication success or failure drives both war and peace because communication is all about connection.

Not coincidentally, the word *communication* comes from the same root as *common, community,* and *communion.* Disputes, and ultimately wars, result from a failure to see commonality, a failure to rise above apparent differences and act instead on the inescapable reality that, while we are individuals, we are also one community, locally and globally.

The reality of our living together in a single community is more critical to humanity's survival than ever. With the explosion of electronic and digital technology, **Realizing** mass media, global merchandising, and resource con- **commonality** sumption, the pace of life grows ever faster and more **will decide** obviously interrelated. A financial crisis in one small **humanity's** nation can unsettle the whole world economy. People **survival.** maintain e-mail friendships – and terrorist conspiracies – around the globe. Stocks are traded 24 hours a day. News travels instantly. Ideological crusades are mobilized overnight. The identical type of coffee or hamburger can be purchased in nearly every country. Epidemics cross oceans and borders at the speed of a jet plane. Air pollution blows freely from one country and continent to the next. Global climate change is, indeed, global.

The ease and speed of modern transportation and communication connect us and also separate us. I enjoy maintaining contact with people all over the world through e-mail. I recognize, however, that these are not intimate connections. In fact, Most of us have grown increasingly isolated, tied to our cell phones, computers, home entertainment systems, and anonymous shopping malls.

People still gather together for holidays and celebrations. But these are special occasions rather than everyday life.

In former times and in more traditional settings, people lived more closely connected. Communication required direct contact. People in neighborhoods, villages, and smaller cities knew each other. Spirituality was inseparable from everyday life. Entertainment was live and lively. Shopping brought maker and buyer together. Extended families lived under the same roofs. Human interrelationships were more direct and apparent.

Not long ago I spent time in an impoverished developing country, where I experienced a vibrancy and social intimacy far beyond what I'm used to in the West. Much of life there takes place on the street. Most people can only afford cheap meals prepared by vendors operating on the sidewalk. Families and friends sit on little stools around small plastic tables, eating together in lively animated groups. Similarly, instead of isolating themselves in massive hunks of steel cars, they rely on bicycles and motorbikes, open to the air, visible and more intimately connected to their surroundings and fellow travelers.

I'm not romanticizing lower standards of living. The cities I visited in that country are also noisy, polluted, and widely unsanitary, and like every society people there have plenty of their own problems. But nor am I idealizing our own so-called rich and advanced lifestyle. We pay a big price for all of our luxury, technology, and ease. One part of that cost is increasing isolation.

Fortunately, that's not the end of the story.

Nurturing your powers

Regardless of how modern life seems to separate us, we remain inextricably interconnected and interdependent. Everything we do affects everything and everyone else. We may not realize our connections, but they manifest themselves at every instant.

All religions one way or another recognize interconnectedness. This fundamental reality of life isn't a mystical or magical idea. Science, too, has shown that nothing, not even the smallest particle, exists separately, in isolation. Everything interacts. Every cause has an effect, and every effect affects everything else in turn. Reality is a ceaseless, endless web of interdependence and connection.

We express connection through communication, and not just in conveying information or convincing people to do something. There are times to convey information, and there are times to convince. But communication goes deeper: communication happens when we tap into our instinctive faculties for finding and creating connections between ourselves and others. Call it compassion, understanding, or love: communication is relationship.

Communication is relationship.

A few years ago, I set out to teach workshops on writing and business communication, which ultimately transformed into this book. In the course of researching the subject, I discovered a glut of books packed with all sorts of technical guidance, rules, and exercises. I didn't want to produce yet another textbook. Instead, I contemplated for some time my own experience, trying to extrapolate what talents I seem to have that enabled me to build a successful career as a professional writer and communications consultant in a competitive environment.

Eventually I boiled these skills or tools down to the ten basic powers described in the following pages. Through subsequent experience using them in lectures and workshops, I'm convinced that these ten powers, because they derive from inborn talents, can help anyone to write and communicate more articulately and effectively. These are fundamental life skills, and as such they will also help you in all aspects of your life to act with greater ease, comfort, and self-confidence.

Although I set out a number of specific techniques you can apply directly to your work and overall life, this book is not a technical manual. You can readily find plenty of those, and later I recommend a few. I also want to emphasize that the ten powers described in this book, as vital and useful as they are, do not lay down a set formula to be blindly followed but, rather, a way of seeing for yourself. Only you can communicate for yourself, and you can.

We communicate by what we do, not merely by what we think, say, or write. Nevertheless, communicating is also something we do.

What I offer here is a guide for reclaiming and nurturing your innate faculties. In doing so, you will find it far easier to create and deliver effective communications in any media and to live life more harmoniously and responsively to the world around you.

Ultimately, we communicate most genuinely by what we do, not merely by what we think, say, or write. There's truth to old sayings like "Easier said than done" and "Words are cheap." Nevertheless, communicating is also something we do.

Although words are representational, not reality itself, they have impact. They affect reality. They shape us. They become us. All the more important, then, that we speak from our heart, from our gut: not in a sentimental way, but to express true meaning and genuine connection with people and with the world inside and outside of ourselves. Our words can and should fit us – they should become us – in the sense that we might say to someone, "That suit is very becoming on you."

As you go through this book you may notice that each chapter echoes things said in the others. The repetition is purposeful, for in the end, the message is quite simple and all encompassing – trust yourself. In truth, you do not really need this book: you already are connected. To communicate and relate with people more fluently, to engage in life more deeply, simply realize your inherent connections and release your inborn talents – let words become you.

I

Trust Nothing

Like life itself, ideas seem to arise from nothing, out of nowhere. This "nothing" is your greatest asset — your insight. Learn to trust your mind's wonderful faculty to sort things out for itself.

JUST DO IT, you tell yourself sharply. Just do it.

You grit your teeth and sigh, Yes, yes, I must. Like the popular athletic slogan said, "Just do it!"

If it were only that easy.

Say, for example, you have the chance of a lifetime to give a presentation at the annual national convention of your professional association. Hundreds of people will be there (including the president of a multinational company you'd love to work for), and you'll be at center stage.

But here you are with less than two days to go, sitting in front of a blank screen, unable to get going, fidgeting with the format, wandering down the hall for a coffee, rechecking your expense account record – in short, doing anything to avoid dealing head on with your top priority. (Believe me, I know the routine well.)

You keep trying to think of a catchy opening or a memorable theme. You've started writing the first paragraph five or so times, only to look at it moments later and think, This is junk. Zap! You erase the whole thing.

On the weekend, you stayed home and sat in front of the computer for several hours straight, determined to break through. Nothing.

Or this scenario: You're facing a big deadline and can't delay any longer; the report is due out tomorrow by noon. No more extensions. You worry that your career depends on getting this done and doing it brilliantly. Your credibility is at stake; you feel on trial before your employers, your peers, your family…and most of all, yourself. You, after all, are your toughest, most damning critic. You're hardest on yourself. (I'm an expert at this, too.) But you just can't get started.

Or yet another situation: You haven't spoken to your sister for seven years, since your last parent died and you fought with each other bitterly over details of the estate. Your brother tried to patch up relations between the two of you, but every attempt failed. At last, you and your sister have agreed to meet over a coffee and try to come to terms. How can the ice be broken, you wonder. How can I explain things without upsetting her again?

Multiply these scenarios a hundred times in a hundred variations: writing a report about a business trip, talking to your best friend about something that's long troubled you but you've kept hidden, creating theme ideas for a promotional campaign, planning a new business strategy, asking your boss for a raise, developing a book idea you've sat on for years, composing a letter telling your lover why you want to break up – or, better yet, why you want to get back together again. But try as hard as you can, you can't think what to say or how to broach the issue.

Over and over again, we all face a void: a void of ideas, inspiration, confidence. Yet this void itself – this emptiness, this nothingness – is your greatest asset and source of insight and inspiration. You only need trust it. Trust "nothing" and learn to use it.

Zeroing in on true nature

I often experience doubts, hesitations, and delays in my own work. During virtually every project inevitably at some point I face a blank screen, when no idea – nothing – seems to appear. Often there's a moment when I lose all hope and think nothing ever will arise and I'll fail.

Over time, I've learned to trust these periods of uncertainty. The anxiety of facing "nothing" has lost its grip over me. I'm not terrified by it. In fact, I've come to see these apparent voids or pauses, when inspiration and solution seem beyond reach, as the most valuable step in the creative, productive process. I've learned to use these pauses, these periods of "nothing," in all aspects of life and work. I've discovered that giving myself a break, a pause in work and effort, is precisely what helps me break through.

The power of nothing most strikingly demonstrates its value for me when I'm asked to develop themes, brand names, or slogans. Somehow, out of nowhere, I must come up again and again with the perfect word or phrase – which is no different from facing any kind of puzzle, predicament, or problem.

Many years ago, for example, the largest property developer in my city was about to celebrate the pouring of the top floor of the company's latest and grandest concrete high-rise office building, a glimmering tower of reflective bronze-tinted glass. Theirs was the first modern tower in the city to be clad wholly in glass; many others followed in succeeding years.

To mark the occasion, called "topping-off" in the construction industry, the company planned to host a breakfast buffet on the top floor, with many dignitaries in attendance. I was asked to create an overall theme for the event, which would be used for everything from the invitations to the food and entertainment.

After reading about the building and the development company's history and talking to its founder and president, I agonized for several days trying to come up with a great slogan. I began to worry, feeling growing panic as nothing seemed right. I was ready to give up. In fact, I did give up. But then, the next morning, my first thought on awakening was "Rise and shine," the age-old call to wake up fresh and positive.

And there it was – an ideal theme, incorporating in just three short words three essential facts about the event: it was a morning affair, it celebrated a tower's rising, and, quite literally, the tower would shine. Plus, the theme was upbeat. How I pulled these three ideas together, I have no idea. It came from "out of the blue," from nowhere, from nothing.

A few years later I received an assignment to develop a marketing theme for a winter program operated by Outward Bound, a notoriously tough outdoor training program. After a period of intensive research, during a moment's pause, a phrase suddenly hit me: "Zero in on your true nature." Like the prior example, these few words together conveyed several key ideas: the winter program would take place in sub-zero conditions, it would happen outdoors in nature, and it would help participants to find themselves, their true nature. Once again, the ideal solution seemed to arise from nowhere.

Immersing yourself in nothing also allows the obvious to be seen — no mean task. More often than not, a problem is best resolved by the most obvious solution, so obvious, in fact, that people don't think of it.

Not too long ago, for example, I was searching for a brand name to cover a family of engineered wood products called oriented strand board (OSB). The panels replace conventional plywood and are manufactured from resin-impregnated strands of wood veneered from fast growing tree species. The strands are layered in alternating directions and then pressed into shape under intense heat and heavy pressure.

The particular type of OSB I was devising a brand for met higher performance standards for specific construction applications. Competitors had already trademarked seemingly every conceivable brand name for similar products. So when the word *durastrand* popped into my head, I thought at first that combining *strand* with *dura* (as in *durable* or *enduring*) was too obvious; surely it must already be registered. But it was so obvious that apparently no one had thought of it. And it arose from nowhere, from nothing.

Can't "just do it"?

To see how to use the power of "nothing" in your own life and work, let's take a closer look at the blank screens and blank minds we all encounter time and time again.

Often, when faced with a tough assignment, we hesitate, delay, avoid, and fool ourselves by making various excuses – at least I do. But no matter what we do, we can't break through. What's going on? Why can't we think of an answer, a solution, a theme? What are we avoiding? What are we afraid of? Is it just failure, or something bleaker?

There must be a way to do it, some trick. Maybe we just need to act more boldly, more decisively, more aggressively.

On and on these thoughts go, as we belittle ourselves or hide from the discomfort that avoidance itself causes, leading to more avoidance and unease. Eventually, for most of us, we do get the job done somehow, typically in a last-minute rush. But it's a painful process, and the quality of the result usually reflects the pain and panic in which it was produced.

We assume that to break through such blockages we must take action. When something's not happening, we think it's because we're not acting aggressively enough. We're too passive, too indecisive, too weak. The literal or figurative blank screen must be filled, regardless of our doubts or hesitancy. So just get on with it, we tell ourselves. Just do it. The report needs to be drafted now. Just do it.

"Just doing it" is wise advice, generally speaking. Spontaneity along with the self-confidence it requires is a healthy behavior. But when we're truly stuck, it's because we can't just do it; or, more accurately, we don't feel we can. The resulting circular predicament is similar to depression: even if we know we're depressed and must pull ourselves out of it, how can we do so acting under the influence of the very malaise itself?

To extract ourselves from such predicaments, we need to examine the apparent contradiction between activity and inactivity. Let's look first at our faith in activity.

Time's not wasted

Most of us believe that in order to make things, create things, or fix things, our mind and body must be consciously active. If there's no activity, nothing's happening. And out of nothing, nothing will ever arise.

Recently, a friend was complaining that he was way behind in writing his PhD thesis. He knew he had to get going now and couldn't put it off any longer. All of this inactivity was getting him nowhere, he complained. It was a waste of time.

Activity happens continuously whether we think so or not. Even doing nothing is a form of activity.

True, every moment is precious. But every moment occurs regardless of whether we think we're actively filling it or not. In truth, time cannot be wasted; it merely passes. Similarly, activity happens continuously whether we think so or not. Even doing nothing is a form of activity.

Nevertheless, apparent inactivity scares us. We think we must be losing out on getting something or getting somewhere if we're not actively pursuing it and steadily making progress. And if there's one thing we want, especially in the Western world, it's getting what we need or want and, most important, getting it now. Whether it's fast food, quick trips, instant e-mail, beating the red light, or sex on demand, we expect our needs and desires to be satisfied on call, twenty-four hours a day. When anything breaks down, we get angry and frustrated. Life should be easy and convenient. What's civilization about, after all, if not convenience and comfort?

If for any reason things turn out too difficult and get us down from time to time, or over a long time, at least we can take antidepressants to smooth out the edges; or anti-anxiety pills when we feel over stressed. A shocking number of people seem to be taking these mood-helpers at some time or another (I have a supply of my own), often telling others why they should be taking them, too. Evidently, even happiness ought to be readily available on demand. Discomfort is, quite simply, unacceptable, and modern medicine has stepped in to cure such ills.

I wouldn't be surprised if someday we'll be able to take a pill or a shot to get us through creative blockages as well as depression. No more woes about the blank screen. The moment we feel uncertain about what to do or say or write, we'll just take a walk to our friendly pharmacy.

Come to think of it, there is a drug people have been using for centuries to deal with writer's block. Liquor has greased many a work of fiction, and notorious drunken rampages and stupors have been celebrated as if the illustrious authors were heroes, their outrageous behavior the laughable byproduct of creative genius.

Drugs regardless, facing the blank screen and its accompanying pain fly in the face of everything we've come to expect from a modern, successful, happy life. Feeling uncertain, avoiding resolution, we find ourselves staring at nothing. No answer, no solution, no ideas, no breakthrough. Nothing. And it's terrifying, for nothing is scarier than nothing. Where do we go? What do we do? Why do anything?

Nothing makes sense; more accurately, nothing makes *no* sense. The ultimate nothing is the annihilation and oblivion of death itself. No time, no place, no me. The final, utterly terrifying blank screen.

All of this fear and uncertainty adds up to a great deal of wasted energy and wasted spirit. But the saddest thing of all is that we're deluding ourselves with misguided fear. For when it comes to creativity and insight, "nothing" is your best friend.

Maybe you haven't gotten to know your friend yet or learned how to draw on its power. "Nothing" can be your greatest source of ideas, solutions, understanding, and, above all, self-confidence – if you know how to see it and use it.

So what is this *nothing?*

Learn to make friends with "nothing."

Brains need food

Many years ago, a friend gave me a little book that dates back to 1940 called *A Technique for Producing Ideas,* written by James Webb Young, a pioneer in the modern American advertising industry. It's still in print (published by McGraw-Hill), and I recommend you get hold of it. The book surprised me not because it told me something I didn't already know, but because it described an internal process – or faculty - I'd intuitively come upon in my own early work writing copy and developing themes for advertising and other media. I hadn't seen this knack for creativity as something special (and it isn't), but merely as an instinctive way to think and work.

Here, based on my own experience, is my take on this process, which I call the power of insight.

In the first step, you gather material about the subject you're dealing with by conducting research, asking
questions, analyzing the audience if you need to communicate something, and so forth. In this focused form of
investigation, the scope is defined narrowly by the subject
at hand and the directions you've received or set out for
yourself.

*Ideas and solutions materializing
from the subconscious level... arise
from your mind's great network of
wired connections.*

In an often forgotten part of research, however, you
also build up the information you glean from every-
where in the natural course of living your life, through
reading, travel, talk, observation, and contemplating the
world. In other words, by continually feeding your mind
you expand the pool of material you can draw on at any
time, not just to suit one particular situation. The more
you feed your mind, the more rich the neural connections become. As a result, ideas and solutions materializing from the subconscious level seem to surface from out
of nowhere, from nothing. In fact, they arise from your
mind's great network of wired connections.

**Feed your mind
with diverse
experiences.**

Our brains function like computers but with vastly
more scope and scale, operating around the clock. To stay
healthy, alive, and creative, our brains need a constant
supply of nourishment, of information in the widest sense.
Ideas arise when the elements of all this material interact.

All we do is recombine them in new ways, insights form-
ing like planets coalesced by gravity from loose matter.
Our capacity to perceive new relationships – new possibilities for combination – shapes our creativity. If, instead,
we narrow our focus, allowing in only a narrow range of
exposure, we denigrate one of our greatest resources: the
natural wisdom gained through life experience.

In other words, "get a life," as the saying goes, and keep   Remain curious
at it. If you want to work insightfully and effectively, live   throughout life.
a full life rich in diverse experience. This doesn't mean
you have to travel widely, read tons of books and journals,
or attend every event. It means that you open yourself
up fully to the experiences that transpire in life, whether
lived in a small city, a great metropolis, or the country-
side, or whether traveling the world or just exploring
your own neighborhood. Life is buzzing all around you,
like radio signals filling the air. Open yourself to every
frequency. Experience and respond to what's happening
in the present. Remain curious throughout life.

Ideas surface

In the second step of the creative process, you "chew up"
all the stuff you've fed into your brains, both the specific
information you've investigated and the broader range of
knowledge you've gathered in leading a multifaceted life.
As you consciously work over all this material, jot down
ideas or insights that arise, think of ways to organize or
handle your subject, and perhaps develop a tentative outline or approach.

But don't get bogged down or tied to any particu
lar answer or solution at this point. For then comes the
most important, but typically undervalued or ignored,
step – doing nothing. Young described this as a period
of incubating or digesting the food you've taken in and

masticated. After a great meal, you don't need to activate your stomach so that it does its work; it just does it. Similarly, you don't need to think about your mind's processing all the material you've gathered; it just does it. The mind "stomach" works like crazy, around the clock. But at your conscious level it may seem like nothing. And *nothing* is how I refer to this digestive process.

Don't try to make your mind work things out. So, in fact, nothing is not nothing. Nothing is actually seething with activity. Only you don't have to be active in the ordinary sense for this activity to transpire. Indeed, if you try to make your mind *act* active, it won't work – just like the old saying, "A watched kettle doesn't boil." Once your mind's been primed with information, all you need do is trust its wonderful faculty to sort things out for itself.

You do have to give yourself a break, however, to let this nothing happen. But unfortunately, as I said earlier, our society is so addicted to instant satisfaction and the necessity for active action that very few of us stop from time to time and let nothing work its magic. Most of us are afraid to stop, afraid that literally nothing will come forth.

People generally assume that the great insights and breakthroughs of genius – like the imaginative creations of Leonardo da Vinci, Newton's realization of gravity, or Einstein's theory of relativity – emerged only when these lofty individuals actively engaged their minds, consciously processing and controlling their thoughts like a technician programming a supercomputer. But, as so many "geniuses" have themselves testified, their breakthrough ideas came from "nowhere."

Archimedes in Ancient Greece stepped into his bathtub and suddenly realized how, by determining an object's displacement of fluid, its relative density could be calculated – a problem he'd long struggled to resolve.

"Eureka!" he's said to have shouted. "I've found it." Or, from another perspective, the breakthrough found him. In his case it literally flooded over him.

As mentioned above, the nowhere or nothing that such breakthroughs come from isn't really a void. Nothing isn't nothing. It's the rich, virtually infinite multidimensional time and space your mind occupies. Instead of restricting yourself to a limited sense of self that sees everything else as separate, let go of this narrow identity and embrace the whole universe of things and ideas and beings. Rather than cut yourself off, allow your mind to wander freely – and also to rest in quiet. And lo and behold, creative ideas and solutions to problems suddenly rise to the surface of your consciousness.

Rely on ideas emerging from "out of the blue."

Once your mind's been primed with information, all you need do is trust its wonderful faculty to sort things out for itself.

Certainly Archimedes and all the other great geniuses had to go through the steps of studying, thinking, digesting, and conscious imagining. They worked long and hard. But their creative breakthroughs came in a flash, suddenly, at unexpected moments – during a bath, a walk, a moment's pause, waking up in the middle of a dream, in the midst of making love.

The same is true for all us lesser – but, in fact, equal – human beings. It's true for me and for you. You have your own genius and beautiful mind. You create in the same fashion. Your breakthroughs and ideas are no less than those of the greats like Einstein and Leonardo. But you, too, need to take a pause in order for your eurekas to emerge, rather than keep banging your head against the wall (or the computer screen), struggling for insight. Insight happens of its own accord. All you need do is trust your inherent faculties.

Taking a pause

Ironically, you can take action to cultivate your faculty for using inaction. Or, to be more precise, you can practice giving yourself the space in which nothing can do its magic – because it's not magic. It's your inborn power of insight.

Allow yourself a period of rest, of nothing, during which your mind can process, refresh itself, and – eureka! – come up with new ideas and insights.

Find your own way to cultivate "nothing."

People have their own ways of doing this; discover what works best for you. Some people practice one form or another of meditation or contemplation, giving themselves set periods to take a break. Through breathing consciously, reciting a mantra, mentally scanning your body, or using some other device, you can allow yourself to gradually let go of the usual things that preoccupy your conscious mind and restrict you from opening up to the broader universe, to things as they are inside you, outside you, and interconnected. A teacher or formal training can help you learn how to do this, but ultimately you must find your own way.

Instead of practicing meditation as such, you can also experience your mind settling and opening when you go for a walk, run, or bike ride, work in the garden, sit in a bath, or play basketball with friends. There's no end to the means you can use to create the time and space to allow yourself a period of rest, of nothing, during which your mind can process, refresh itself, and – eureka! – come up with new ideas and insights.

But I'm too busy, you tell yourself. I don't have time. I've got to find the solution now!

Yes, we all find ourselves in such spots; they're inevitable. The question then becomes, how can you take time to meditate or play or garden when you have no time, when the deadline is now, or ten minutes from now.

Given even the tightest deadline, however, you can still take just a moment's pause, and often that alone may lead to the very breakthrough you need to move forward. Time and time again, I've turned away from my computer – or ages ago, so it seems, from my paper pad – and gotten up to make a cup of coffee, go for a swim, or take a shower, and in that pause the answer or the idea suddenly sprang to mind. Over the years I've grown to trust this pause, this moment if a moment is all I have, to go into nothing. It works, but you must learn to trust it and cultivate it.

Take even a moment's break.

Here's a parallel example that might convince you. No doubt you've had the experience of trying to recall someone's name or some other familiar fact, but you can't remember it as hard as you try. In fact, the harder you try, the harder it gets. "It's on the tip of my tongue," you say, but to no avail. And then, just when you finally give up the struggle and move on to doing or thinking about something else, the name or fact suddenly pops into your head. That's it: that's letting "nothing" do its thing.

The more you tap into the power of nothing, the more you'll find that these unstructured pauses leading to lucidity happen continually. Even when you think you're being active, in actual fact your consciousness is working like a swinging door: one moment you're just receiving or processing, but the next instant you're actively thinking or looking or feeling. The door opens, the door closes – effortlessly, fluently.

This ongoing process, the natural rhythm of life and consciousness, is so constant, so subtle, that you're not aware of it. But as you become more adept at allowing yourself to delve into the non-active as well as the active facet of your consciousness, you will find that ideas and solutions pop out, not just when you're working on them, or even when taking a pause, but at any moment.

Sometimes a breakthrough happens when you first encounter a new situation or problem. I often find that a creative solution – such as a theme, organizing concept, or brand name – pops into my head while I'm first being briefed for a project.

One time, for instance, a client who owned several chains of restaurants explained that one chain with a medieval theme – lots of armor, ribs, and beer – was actually patronized by a more upscale market and thus required a more sophisticated theme. Suddenly I said, "Hey, why not move out of the Middle Ages and into the Renaissance?" He loved the idea, even though he didn't fully understand that the Renaissance was an age of enlightenment following the Middle Ages.

I've learned, though, not to jump to conclusions, blurt out my idea on the spot, and impress a client with my amazing (or harebrained) insight. Instead, I jot the thoughts down whenever they occur, giving myself time (yes, another pause) to verify my ideas and allow time to pass and judgment to form. Moreover, it's not easy to charge a fair price for something like a theme or brand name if it looks like I only spent a moment of billable time to come up with it. In fact, it takes a countless amount of time to come to trust nothing and cultivate the process. It also takes time to build the greater pool of knowledge that feeds the ability for these breakthroughs to come from nothing, "out of thin air." (Perhaps I should bill for all the time I spend meditating, swimming, biking, reading magazines, and talking to friends.)

Record ideas as they arise; check them later.

To cultivate the power of nothing, develop a practice of taking regular breaks, gardening, walking, or doing whatever something or nothing works for you. Build in pauses at various stages of your work, not just at the last moment when you're desperate for ideas or solutions and time's running out. Take advantage of nothing at any time and discover a realm of insight you never imagined you possessed.

Build in pauses throughout your work.

Give yourself a break. Just do it.

Like communication itself, this "nothing" is your birthright. It's a place, more accurately a power, you can go to and draw on again and again for the rest of your life. All of us have an inherent ability to tap into this power. You need only allow yourself the time and space to submerge into your mind's natural connections to the wider universe as a source of insight, clarity, and ideas. Give yourself a break. Just do it.

But remember, it doesn't end with eureka. After a burst of insight, you must next do the more detailed work of elaborating your ideas or solutions and then communicating them in an appropriate form. And this I cover in later chapters.

YOUR STORY

Each chapter concludes with a brief writing exercise in which you can reflect on how you personally relate to the chapter's topic. After you've done the exercise, feel free to submit it to the book's website www.WordsBecomeYou.com. Then spread the word and tell your friends and coworkers about the book and the website.

For this chapter, describe in one or two short paragraphs a memorable experience when an idea or a solution to a problem suddenly popped into your head. What was the problem or issue you were dealing with, what were you doing (or not doing) when the idea or insight appeared "out of the blue" (from nothing), and how did it solve the problem?

2

Hear Everything, Know Anything

We communicate and function best when we perceive things just as they are. To get the information you need, engage in genuine conversation, understand your audience, and, above all, remain curious about life. Be confident that anything is knowable.

MOST COMMUNICATION EXPERTS stress the importance of listening. Communication cannot be one way, they say: you must listen to others if you wish to get your own message across. Communication is the art of listening, not just expressing.

This is good advice as far as it goes. But from my experience it doesn't go far enough. Listening by definition means to give close attention and make an effort to hear. But who is the *who* who's giving close attention and making the effort? Clearly, it's *me*. I am here, distinct, listening to someone else who's talking – *you*. You are the speaker; I am the listener. In other words, you and I are separate. Therefore, I must make a concerted effort and direct myself to listen actively.

Yet in telling ourselves to listen, do we really hear?

Not exactly. If I'm honest with myself, I'll admit that much of the time I'm supposedly listening I'm actually receiving much of what's said through my own filters. It's as if when another person talks I'm hearing my own voice commenting steadily on what I'm listening to, rather than simply hearing it and taking it in as it is. This habit of filtering what I hear has built up over a lifetime of habitual and often subtle social interaction, shaped by little fears or insecurities and by a desire to fit in or fend off.

Is this true for you, as well? How much of what you receive is interpreted through your own preconceptions, assumptions, and prejudices? In short, are you listening not so much to others but mostly to yourself? Don't be embarrassed to admit it; nearly all of us listen in this limited fashion.

When you're present, all of your sensory organs receive stimuli naturally and uncorrupted.

Hearing is different. Hearing is our inherent function for perceiving what's actually happening around us. Hearing simply means being present. When you're present, all of your sensory organs receive stimuli naturally and uncorrupted, without your having to actively engage your senses.

That's why when you put your hand into scalding hot water you don't need to direct yourself to stop and think, Is this hot? Your hand knows it instantly. And so do you. And in that instant, you, your hand, and the hot water are connected, not separate. The moment you start thinking,

This water is really hot, the connection is broken: you and the water are separate. Of course, by that time you've instinctively jerked your hand out of the water, before your thinking got in the way.

The same holds true for real listening – hearing – or real looking – seeing. In fact, you don't need to actively engage your brain or any of your five senses; you need only be openly present to connect with things just as they are. When you speak with me, your ears hear my words and your eyes see my body language without your having to instruct yourself to listen and pay attention. Perception occurs spontaneously, and through perception we learn, inquire, and understand.

MY STORY

Helping others hear

I never set out intentionally to cultivate the innate faculty of hearing. But its value has been driven home to me again and again – and perhaps most noticeably when, in the process of inquiry, I've had to help others to hear one another.

Back in the early 1980s I was asked to assist a committee to write a report about compensating injuries caused by automobile accidents. The committee's mission resulted from a tragic case where a young mother was rendered a quadriplegic in a crash that she herself caused. A senior politician was shocked to learn that the mother and anyone else suffering catastrophic injuries received little or no compensation for their losses if they were at fault in causing the crash, even if due to a minor technicality.

This is because nearly all jurisdictions in North America work on the fault principle. Injured people are almost entirely compensated not through their own insurance but by successfully suing the alleged wrongdoer and receiving compensation from that person's insurance. If you're the one at fault, you're out of luck.

The politician asked a public agency to set up a committee to recommend a new system. Twelve representatives from diverse interests were appointed, including lawyers, insurance executives, independent agents and adjusters, and consumer advocates. After deliberating for nearly three years, the committee had failed to reach a consensus but was under growing pressure to issue its findings. They'd been listening to each other and trying so hard for so long to reach an agreement that they had stopped really hearing one another.

Knowing instinctively it would be problematic to write a document for a committee, I decided that instead of meeting with them as a whole I would interview each of the twelve members individually. As I listened to *(heard)* each of their impressions and opinions, I realized that the group indeed had a consensus, but that they hadn't been able to hear it talking among themselves.

After completing the interviews and other research, I wrote the book-length report, including a section on minority views appended to each chapter. I suggested that the committee not review the draft collectively at a meeting, but that each member independently note down any objections or desired changes on his or her copy.

Once I received all twelve, marked copies, I revised the draft – surprisingly few changes were required – and resubmitted it. And that was it. The committee was astounded at how readily the task was completed. They relaxed, communicated more openly as a group, and the report was soon released.

When I told this story to a friend who was a leading expert in labor negotiations, he said, somewhat surprised, "You used single-text bargaining. How did you know that technique? It breaks many log jams."

When opposing sides in a labor dispute cannot reach agreement, my friend explained, the impasse can often be broken if a mediator submits a proposed agreement in writing. The mediator asks the sides not to accept or reject the report nor discuss it as a group, but rather to independently write down any changes they want.

This process, which I'd intuitively employed with my committee, helps people to find common ground. Instead of dwelling on their differences, they discover that their opinions and desires overlap and coincide. But often it takes an outside person, a mediator or facilitator, to help people break their habitual patterns, open up, and begin to hear one another.

Openness makes you strong

Opening up your sensory perceptions doesn't always come easily, especially when you've grown accustomed to ignoring them. You can't exactly tell yourself to open up, because the moment you do you've created a kind of self-instruction, a filter. When you're listening to other people through your own filters – judging what's being said or instructing yourself how to listen and react – you're not being open, and you're not really hearing. The more you let go of your personal filters, the more directly you perceive and respond to the world around you as it is. If others are sad, you feel their sadness. If others are angry, you feel their anger.

So how can you do this? By not trying too hard. Just be there. Be here. Be present. Trust yourself and your senses. Perception is innate.

You might worry that this kind of listening is too passive: that if you're busy receiving information without actively filtering or judging its content and significance, you're opening yourself up not to genuine perception but to misinterpretation or even potential danger. So much information is crowding in on our lives, it feels like a wild jungle. If we're not carefully watching ourselves and weeding through all the stuff, sorting out "friend from foe" as it were, we might get fooled or we might get hurt. Or so we might fear.

The more you let go of your personal filters, the more directly you perceive and respond to the world around you as it is.

True hearing does not, however, turn you into a gullible or vulnerable victim, believing and endorsing everything you hear. In hearing with an open mind, instead of getting lost in judgments and thoughts, you strengthen your center of gravity and respond more appropriately to whatever situations you encounter. For example, if someone is consumed by sadness, you feel it but you don't lose yourself in it. You hear, but your response is grounded in your own natural wisdom. Communication is not merely hearing truly; it's also responding truly.

Think of it like breathing. When you take in a breath, you consume the air. But the air also consumes you. Molecules of oxygen penetrate through your lungs, enter your bloodstream, and occupy every cell of your being. You are no longer strictly the same person. And, in turn, when you exhale you manifest your changed being. The air becomes you. Eating works similarly, as does interacting with the world and communicating with others. In hearing and responding, you reflect to some measure the other person, and the other person reflects you.

Interacting openly doesn't make you vulnerable to people bludgeoning you, literally or figuratively. If particular individuals do present a threat, understanding where they're coming from and how they perceive things gives you added power to respond from strength. Effective spies don't find out what they're supposed to discover; they discover what's really going on. And good leaders don't act on what they want to believe.

In other words, sensing things without fear functions as a vigorous, active form of engagement. Closing yourself, listening only to what you're prepared to hear, comes from fear. Operating from fear puts you in a weak and vulnerable position; openness engenders confidence and strength.

That all sounds very nice, you might reasonably think. But I have a job to do; I have to find out about something and communicate it now. What am I suppose to do in the meantime before I'm "perfect" and able to hear and respond a hundred percent?

Forget about perfection.

Don't wait until you're perfect. If I did, I would get nowhere. Like everyone else I'm imperfect. I don't hear fully; I still have far too many filters operating. But rather than beat yourself up about limitations, relax and evolve

step by step toward greater receptivity. Every little bit you
unlock your innate senses, becoming more fully present,
the more you perceive things just as they are, and the
more effectively you respond. Here are some tips on how
to hone your hearing skills.

Sensing things as they are

Your innate skill for direct hearing and perception empowers you to conduct genuine inquiry – to learn what
you need to know in order to connect with others successfully and handle any situation that arises. Whether you're
coping with a serious disease, facing a major challenge at
work, writing a report for your company, or composing
a love letter to someone you're deeply attracted to, the
more directly you understand those you wish to reach out
to the sharper your response. Knowing your audience is
as important as knowing your subject.

In the realm of communication, the first step is gathering information. Information is food. Without food, the
brain can't process or understand. As explained in the
previous chapter, the brain requires nourishment.

Nourish your brain with information.

In my experience, organizations and businesses as well
as individuals frequently try to communicate without
first gathering sufficient facts, impressions, and other information – in other words, whatever is needed to understand a topic or issue, formulate objectives, appreciate the
audience, and look at competing messages. Even when
businesses acknowledge the importance of market intel-
ligence, they may skip over it in the rush to complete an
assignment or under pressure from other priorities.

Just as an athlete or physical laborer requires nourishment to build strength and gain the energy needed to
perform, you require information and understanding in
order to communicate. I don't mean to suggest that it's a

linear path: information does not necessarily lead automatically to effective communication. But without first
hearing and seeing things as they are, you won't know
where to head.

Getting good briefings has formed the cornerstone of
my own inquiries. At the start of an assignment, I meet
with the key people involved and others at all levels of the
organization. I try to go to the top because senior executives, at least in theory, ought to know the big picture.
But I also spend time with people at other levels – middle
management, on the shop floor, out in the field – because
they often remain in closer touch with the down-to-
earth realities that shape a situation or story. Sometimes
they're a bit cynical about things, but contrary views also
provide insight.

Get good briefings from the start.

Engaging conversation

In conducting interviews and briefings, I've cultivated a
knack for hearing that I refer to as *skilled naivety*. By this I
mean approaching topics as if they're totally new, whether
they are or not. And if I'm honest with myself, I have to
admit that I'm fairly ignorant about most things. There's
always someone who knows more than I do about any
given topic. So, when inquiring into a subject, don't pretend even to yourself that you already know everything
about it. Remain innocent-like, willing to learn about
the subject totally fresh.

Capitalize on your "naivety."

Before conducting an interview or any other kind of
inquiry, begin by developing a list of questions. These
questions should relate directly to the matter at hand. But
don't make the classic mistake of interviewing people
strictly on the narrow basis of your questions or checklist,
whether on paper or in your head. It bores or intimidates
people when they're grilled from a list. Leave that to the

torture chamber. While interviewing someone, remain open and, in turn, open up your source.

After developing my list of questions, I usually check if I've covered the fundamentals aspiring journalists have long been taught to pursue: Who, What, Where, Why, When, and How. I remember back in junior high school taking a journalism class and being indoctrinated in asking the five Ws and one H. It's funny, they seemed so simpleminded at the time. But they work: they invariably point to all the necessary lines of inquiry.

Toward the end of most interviews, I quickly review the Who's and What's, plus my list of questions, confirming that I've covered everything. If something hasn't been covered, I go back to it as a sort of afterthought and ask something like, "So why are you actually planning this campaign?" or "Where are your principal markets?" Note, though, that I rarely refer to my checklist – or go through the Who-What questions – until near the end of an interview, using them as a crosscheck to make sure I've covered all the bases.

During the interview itself or any kind of meeting, behave as if it's a real human encounter – after all, it is. You're getting to know someone and learning about something he or she cares about and has intimate knowledge of. In other words, every interview and meeting is a genuine conversation.

Conversations typically do not follow a narrow, linear path. They wander about, with two or more voices flowing back and forth and through one another. Tapping into this apparent randomness unlocks the door to your power of perception and the art of hearing.

If, instead, you insist on adhering strictly to your list of questions – your prior personal perspective – you may not hear what other people are actually telling you, including insights they might not even be aware of themselves.

Recheck your questions at the end of an interview.

Go with the flow.

In fact, when someone shifts the topic or says something slightly off key or confusing, if you respond to this shift, you will often uncover the most important details or insights to what you're seeking. But if you're not hearing, if instead you're listening from your own perspective and mostly just hearing yourself, you'll likely miss the cue. (Responding to unexpected twists and turns of all kinds offers so much potential benefit that I give it a chapter of its own.)

Every interview and every meeting is a genuine conversation.

When interviewing people or otherwise investigating a topic, it helps to think a bit like a child hearing a bedtime story. Children love hearing stories read to them again and again, even when they already know every line before you say it. With each reading, the story comes alive again, and the child experiences the drama more keenly. Expectation of what's coming next feeds the richness of the experience.

Hear things always as if it's the first time.

As we grow older we experience similar feelings when we watch a film more than once or see the same classic plays or operas many times. There's always a kernel of hope that somehow, this time, at last, Romeo and Juliet will escape doing themselves in.

Talking to people and getting information should remain similarly hopeful and fresh. If you conduct interviews or other forms of inquiry with a cynical and skeptical view that you've heard it all before, you won't hear or learn anything new. Genuine communication is destroyed. (Journalism often disappoints me for this very reason. There's far too little intelligent naivety; a propensity for cynicism and character assassination replaces curiosity.)

Allow yourself instead to remain curious and receptive. Each time you set out to learn about a topic, treat it as new, unexplored territory. Each time you interview or meet with someone, hear a different story. Even if the story becomes repetitive, remember that repetition itself contains meaning, alerting you to both patterns and anomalies.

You should also develop a sense for noting what is not said. Often people consciously or unconsciously leave out the most important or revealing information. Maybe they're avoiding it or ignoring it. Either way, don't miss anything, including "nothing." By remaining curious instead of skeptical or cynical you will more likely catch the missing points as well as those spoken.

None of this is to suggest that you should behave meekly or passively when inquiring into a subject or conversing with people. Rather, you should maintain a sharp focus, hearing acutely, your senses fully attuned, ready at every moment to pursue a twist or turn in the conversation or research. People need to be challenged as well as believed. For example, I often question my clients about their purpose, objectives, and strategies, probing to see the differences even if they don't — especially if they don't.

Be curious, alert to both what is and isn't said.

Probe for purpose

Early on in most projects I ask my clients to identify the central purpose of whatever it is I'm going to create for them, be it an ad campaign, a communications plan, a theme or brand, a brochure, or even a whole book. Very often, people can't explain their central purpose very clearly, either because they haven't thought it through or they just can't boil things down that precisely.

If that happens to you when you're trying to understand a communication project or other task, don't let it stop you. Seek the purpose regardless, knowing that eventually you will figure out the answer, even if others can't. This exercise itself might turn out to be your most valuable contribution. Besides, without understanding the guiding purpose, I find for myself that I can't do a decent job.

To get at a clear sense of purpose, begin by asking what the project's key objectives are, trying to get whomever it is you're working with – including yourself – to reduce this to three to five items. Most people find it easier to identify specific objectives than one essential, overall purpose. Mind you, objectives are not the same as an overriding purpose. But don't let that hold you back. Objectives are typically narrower and more specific.

Begin by identifying specific objectives.

Nor are objectives the same as strategies. This distinction is widely misunderstood, and clarifying it (at least in your own mind) can reveal a great deal about a project. An objective is something the relative achievement of which can be measured, though not necessarily statistically. Achieving some objectives, such as creating or expanding a market for a product, can be measured. Others, like building understanding, are more subjective. Measurement often takes the form of perception and judgment. No matter. Objectives can be measured. Strategies, on the other hand, are the methods or means whereby objectives are achieved. Objectives are reasons for doing things; strategies are how the things are done.

When I ask people to tell me their objectives, usually they set out their strategies. For example, a client might say the objective is to publish sharper, more exciting, or more informative advertising. Well, that's a noble intent and very aesthetic. But what's the objective? Is it to feel better about themselves and their product (which might have some merit)? Or do they have no reason at all, just feeling they need to replace old material?

Instead of accepting strategies or vague desires as objectives, probe gently and ask yourself or others a simple question like, "So what is the reason for doing better ads?" or "What problems have been encountered with the old versions?" The objective in this case might be something like, we need to attract a more hip market, an older market, or a market in a new region, or we need to explain something new about our product.

To take an altogether different example, say you're a plumber, and a client asks you to extend a water supply line from one part of the kitchen to another. You could do the job without knowing more, but would you know exactly how to do it — at what height, for example, the pipe should end up? What's the objective? If the client tells you, however, that he needs the water line because he's planning to hook up a refrigerator's automatic ice-maker, now you know how to do the job right.

Pursuing this line of questioning, seeking the reasoning behind a project, though often a labyrinthine process, ultimately reveals the real objectives and hopefully the central purpose as well — in the above example, an easy-to-use kitchen. And only when you know this can you do something that actually helps achieve the objectives. Otherwise, you're merely producing a nice-looking and nice-sounding ad or building a pipe to nowhere. You're using a strategy to achieve a strategy, which doesn't make any sense.

A lack of clear objectives and purpose typifies much of what is said and done these days. Hence, it's hardly surprising that a great deal of the communication filling our airwaves and our mental space doesn't make much sense.

Differentiate between objectives and strategies.

Maybe that's why decibel levels seem to keep rising, making us all hard of hearing. Messages have to be blared at us otherwise we wouldn't bother listening.

If something has been well thought out and executed, however, it need not, metaphorically speaking, be broadcast so loudly to be heard. When imagination arises from real meaning and purpose, your communication will more likely capture people's attention.

Be sure, then, to distinguish at least in your own mind between objectives and strategies, sorting out desires from actions – even if your boss or coworkers don't understand the difference. Often the difference is subtle, but seeing it for yourself promotes inquiry and hearing. Don't give up looking for the answer. Be sensitively aggressive. Hearing, after all, isn't a passive exercise. It's engagement.

When imagination arises from real meaning and purpose, your communication will more likely capture people's attention.

Ignorance is a skill

One key to engaging more fully is not being afraid to appear ignorant. Be the person you genuinely are, not someone trying to impress others with your great knowledge and ability. Little if anything is gained from fooling others, and even less from fooling yourself. You waste energy and lose strength by striving to create impressions rather than simply being yourself.

Early on in my career I began working with highly specialized professionals in fields such as biology, law, engineering, and medicine. They possessed vast amounts of technical knowledge I could never accumulate in my role as a generalist. And yet I had to learn things from them in order to prepare materials that communicated information in their areas of expertise.

Most of us are intimidated by so-called experts. I certainly was. But for whatever reason, I got over this. Just remember that experts have inside knowledge about a particular topic only because that's what they've spent their life studying and working on. You've spent your life doing other things. There's no shame in not knowing something.

Don't be intimidated by "experts."

Besides, what passes as arcane technical knowledge typically consists of simpler ideas elaborated and expressed in more complex and specialized language or vocabulary, often unnecessarily complex and full of jargon. Be confident that, in actual fact, anything can be communicated clearly if you take the time to understand and translate it into ordinary language.

The trick is to remain persistent enough to arrive at an understanding of what the technical and complex language is actually saying. Very often your ignorance will provide the exact tool required to uncover meaning and open up communication.

Here's why. Technical people habitually communicate mostly with their peers, so they develop a specialized language closed to the rest of us. This can go to extremes, where people are saying things that are so obtuse or studying such narrow aspects that they themselves may not fundamentally understand the larger truths. I've found that when I take the time to understand in simpler terms what highly specialized people are trying to communicate, and then I write it clearly, they are astounded.

Often, they suddenly see things clearer in their own field of work.

I remember one of the first times this happened to me, early in my career. I was sitting around a boardroom table with a group of lawyers who were discussing a complicated piece of proposed legislation. I didn't understand the details of what they were talking about, but one particular item seemed confusing. I asked them to clarify it, pointing out to them what seemed inconsistent. They looked at me a little stunned, and the senior lawyer asked, "How did you think of that without being a lawyer?"

By using your ignorance with confidence, you find that virtually anything is knowable. And anything can be communicated.

Simple: by not being afraid to ask "dumb" questions. In an interview or meeting, if someone says something you don't understand, instead of hesitating and fearing that you'll reveal your ignorance if you ask for clarification, say something like, "I'm sorry, I don't quite understand that. I don't really know too much about (whatever the subject is). Could you explain it to me in simpler terms?" You'll be pleasantly surprised that experts and other authorities enjoy doing this, even when you need to keep pushing until you get the clarity you require.

Through this process you can discover how to communicate a subject to a broader audience who, like you, are unfamiliar with it, at least with all its intricacies. Be

Ask questions freely, fearless of showing ignorance.

confident in communication; be confident in life. By using your own ignorance or lack of full understanding, you discover how to express things more clearly. By using your ignorance with confidence, you find that virtually anything is knowable. And anything can be communicated.

Near the end of an interview, I often return to the basics and say something like, "If you could leave only one impression or one essential piece of information with your audience" through your book, report, article, speech, exhibit, whatever, "what would that be?" This deceptively simple question regularly elicits exactly what was sought at the beginning – the big picture, the main message, the core purpose.

At the right moment, zero in on the core purpose.

You could ask the same type of question if your project concerned, say, an environmental study of a river delta. After learning all the objectives and detailed plans, you could ask your manager or the project's sponsors, "If this study could answer only one question or resolve only one problem, what would that be?" Maybe that answer is, how to save the wildlife habitat from encroaching urbanization. Wow! Now that gives definition and purpose.

But you must ask the fundamental question at an opportune moment. If you ask too soon, the person may not be comfortable or loosened up enough yet. At the end, when you understand the subject better yourself, you've gained trust by hearing the person and responding genuinely to twists and turns in the conversation. Then go for the guts.

Know your audience

Whatever method of inquiry you use – interviews, library research, surveys, focus groups, Internet search, telephone calls – you're seeking the level of detailed information required to do your job. Usually, I get most of what I need from interviews. They're easily arranged and they quickly provide the level of detail I need. Sometimes, of course, a greater depth of background information is required. The more you understand the topic at hand, the more comfortable and prepared you are to handle it.

But information is not enough. As well as investigating your topic, you must also consider the intended audience. People frequently attempt to communicate or carry out projects without adequately evaluating the interests and inclinations of those whom they're trying to reach. Even if you're not trying to sell something, consider carefully how to relate to the people concerned. This seems so elementary, but even sophisticated organizations and companies often ignore this critical step.

Relate to your audience's needs and interests.

Without considering your audience, you're shooting in the dark; you're just speaking to yourself.

With marketing or promotion, such inquiries can range from conducting intensive research and surveys to simply stopping and taking the time to think about your audience. Without considering your audience, you're shooting in the dark; you're just speaking to yourself. And it's the same whether you're giving an address, writing a memo, planning a huge advertising campaign, building a subway line through an old neighborhood, establishing an aid program in an impoverished country, or introducing new tax-reporting requirements. Who are you trying to reach out to?

These days people are inundated with information and communication. Audiences are overloaded and overwhelmed. Why should they stop and pay attention to whatever you're trying to tell them or sell them? You may think that you have the most important and valuable thing to express, or that your project will help people immeasurably. But don't expect your enthusiasm to translate into attention, arousal, or support. You must consider first how to create interest, how to relate to others. Or better yet, how to tap into your audience's existing interests.

What works varies so widely according to the circumstances that there's no one answer for how to reach out to people. Each circumstance warrants a different style of interaction, anywhere on a scale from shocking, direct, or surprising, to indirect, obtuse, mellow, or even invisible.

Interact by relating to the circumstances.

Regardless, just use your power of perception: hear others before you attempt to attract their attention or stimulate a response. Consider what's troubling them, what they care about, where they're coming from (their culture, language, customs), and their concerns and needs.

Just as most people fail to distinguish between objectives and strategies when they set out to communicate or achieve an aim, they also confuse what they have to offer with what others want. A worldly wise businessman I know, who once controlled a giant North American retail chain, told me what he considered the secret to his entire success. Early on, as a poor immigrant selling remaindered goods such as retail shelving, he would learn first what a customer's problems were instead of trying to push the merchandise he happened to get his hands on. Then he would show the customer how the product would solve his particular problems. It seems so obviously the right approach, yet it's often forgotten. And it made him very rich at a young age.

Understanding people's needs, problems, and desires is what market research is all about. When time and budget afford it, in-depth research can reveal critical information about the people you wish to reach out to, information that should shape the nature of your communication or other initiative.

We are each unique, whether as individuals, sub-groups, or cultures; but we also have very similar needs and desires

But here I'm going to say something that, on the surface, might seem to contradict everything I just said about understanding others' needs and interests rather than merely what you're trying to say, sell, or do. Also consider other people's thinking by looking into your own mind. Human beings are not as radically different as we think they are. We are each unique, of course, whether as individuals, sub-groups, or cultures; but we also have very similar needs and desires.

> Know others by also looking into your own mind.

I'm amazed at how often I begin to contemplate changing something in my own life – as shallow as searching for a new type of mobile phone or as profound as devoting myself to a particular cause – only to discover that something I think I've come to independently happens to be the latest invention or fad. It's as if we're so wired together and so influenced by the same environment, the same changing patterns, that more often than not we're looking for exactly the same things. And we are.

At our conscious level, just as with the observable universe, we feel like we operate as individual entities, like separate planets. But we're also part of a vast web, a universe of subtle and not-so-subtle links. This holds true for every aspect of life, be it weather patterns, traffic flows, or fashion. A car stopped momentarily on a freeway causes traffic to back up for miles. A shifting weather front in one small region changes storm patterns around the globe. Fashions popular among sub-groups are picked up by major designers and retailers, becoming widespread trends which the sub-groups then break away from, leading to new cycles.

Events transpire like the intersecting waves set off by raindrops on a still lake. Only our universal lake of consciousness and behavior receives untold numbers of drops, with never a moment of stillness other than the stillness of constant change itself.

Getting a life

Just as our environment and lives are inherently linked to the universe at large, so, too, is our ingenuity. Ideas do not emerge in a strictly linear manner, proceeding directly from question to research to answer. The mind's connections are vast, and ideas pop out from its endless, all-encompassing existence.

Accumulate knowledge every day.

So don't make the mistake of focusing your inquiry narrowly on the subject at hand. Broad experience feeds knowledge and creativity. To tune in, hear, create, and communicate, your mind must be steadily enriched not just with the specific information required to do a specific task, but also with a broad range of knowledge accumulated every day and throughout your life. Why limit your brainpower and source of inspiration and understanding when you can draw on the full human experience?

Unfortunately, we live in a busy task-oriented world, a world oriented to immediate satisfaction. Few people afford themselves the luxury of simply taking things in, reading widely, exposing themselves to a diversity of cultures and experiences, and exercising their native curiosity in areas seemingly removed from their day-to-day concerns. The workaday world forces us into pigeon-holes that limit our range of experience and insight.

But the brain requires expansive nourishment to generate "new" ideas because ideas are not, in fact, truly new. Nothing totally new is ever created. New ideas derive not from new matter but from new combinations of what already exists. It's just like the universe's birth, when the basic ingredients for all matter came into being at once. Although matter has changed and recombined endlessly since then, nothing totally new has emerged.

Think of it also like breathing air. Every time you inhale you're not breathing new air but taking in atoms of oxygen breathed by everyone in the past. You're inhaling air previously consumed by Einstein, Leonardo da Vinci, Buddha, Mother Teresa, and also some characters whose air you'd probably rather not share.

Similarly, in the realm of creativity and communication, we consume and rearrange all the myriad of stuff that has gone before and exists here still. This recycling dynamic holds as true for literature and art as for merchandising and popular culture.

Even science, in its steady exploration deeper and deeper into microscopic detail and mathematical probability, and farther and farther out into the infinite reaches of space, seems to rediscover and reiterate principles conceived of in ancient times. Many of the latest theories on time and space and the origin of our universe bear remarkable similarity to age-old spiritual and philosophical conceptions.

I'm not denigrating modern science or human inno-
vation. Indeed, our ability to recombine elements into
original ideas defines the beauty of our humanity.

To fulfill your human nature in all its wonderfully rich
potential, keep an open mind, develop acute hearing, and
feed freely and widely in the realm of perception and experience. Allow your mental synapses to keep firing away,
finding all sorts of interesting new connections and combinations. Hearing, inquiring, creating, communicating
– these are the natural processes of living your everyday,
extraordinary life.

YOUR STORY

Was there ever a time when you had to learn about
a subject completely unknown or new to you? Did
you feel intimidated, uncertain? Describe in one or
two paragraphs how you overcame your uncertainty
and went about understanding the topic? What steps
did you take to get the information you needed; did
you uncover a central purpose to the work; how did
others respond to your finished product? Submit
your story to www.WordsBecomeYou.com.

3

Mind Your Gut

*Pursuing subtle gut reactions can reveal critical information
and prevent serious errors that might otherwise haunt you later.
Learn to pay attention to your sixth sense – your intuition.*

YOU'RE WALKING OUT OF A MEETING heading down
the hall back to your office, feeling slightly disoriented.
Something wasn't quite right about what was discussed at
the meeting – or what wasn't discussed. You feel a little
queasiness in your stomach. Or just a touch dizzy, your
vision a tiny bit fuzzy. Or in some other way, just a bit
odd and unsettled.

Maybe you can't quite remember exactly what it was
that happened – or didn't happen. Whatever it was,
something didn't feel quite right. But you didn't follow
up on it and now you're feeling nervous. Oh well, maybe
it wasn't anything serious, you tell yourself. Though you
can't be sure, you bury the passing unease.

Another time, you're reviewing the final draft of a report you and your group have worked on for months.
You're correcting errors and rewriting a few passages.
While focusing on these straightforward matters, you
skip over something that, just for an instant, struck you as

possibly incorrect or slightly askew. Ignoring it has left in
its wake a twinge of doubt.

Maybe you can't even recall exactly what the item
was. But you know something somewhere was wrong
or slightly off key. Should you go back and check for it
again? There's not much time, you're tired, and you've
worked on this document long enough. Later, when the
report comes out, this apparently minor error comes back
to haunt you. The misunderstanding and doubt it's created threatens to undermine the entire credibility of your
work.

---

*Time after time, we miss or ignore
subtle clues in all areas of our life.*

Or maybe you just missed a glaring typo or misspelling.
If you're a writer or editor like me – or anyone else who
cares about accuracy and the importance of presentation –
missing such an obvious mistake is embarrassing, leaving
you wondering, How could I have let it pass? Why didn't
I take a moment to check the document more carefully?

Such incidents occur frequently. Indeed, they're the
norm. Little instances of doubt and misgiving cross our
minds throughout our working and day-to-day lives:
Buying a pair of tempting, handsome shoes even though I
sensed they didn't quite fit perfectly, later throwing them
out after wearing them only one or two times. Putting
a lot of money into a speculative investment that felt a
tiny bit dubious – and was. Hurting a child's feelings because I ignored her while busy on the phone, discovering
too late that something was seriously troubling her. Not
responding to a parent's seemingly minor ailment that

later proved life threatening. Failing to take caution even though sensing that the driver in the next lane over was behaving erratically, only to be hit by the car moments later as the driver cut into my lane.

Time after time, we miss or ignore subtle clues in all areas of our life. It's as if we're blind or deaf to all but the most glaring or disturbing problems and challenges. Unless something hits us over the head, we tend to overlook it or forget it. Little things, however, can blow way out of proportion; or, more precisely, we fail early on to recognize their true proportion. In missing, ignoring, or avoiding these subtle clues, we're neglecting one of our greatest assets, our sixth sense – the power of intuition.

What I remember most are not the times I've missed these subtle clues, too numerous to recall, but striking examples of when I paid attention and benefited.

MY STORY

Revealing the unexpected

Some time ago I went to a printing plant to inspect the press proofs of a special issue on mild head injury for a magazine I edited for a number of years. Its publication would mark the first time the subject had been dealt with comprehensively and for a diverse readership rather than highly specialized experts.

As I stood there at the printers taking a close look at the proof of one particular brain scan we were including, I felt uneasy about the colors used to identify different types of brain tissue. One marked *marigold* and another *orange* seemed too similar.

Much work had gone into producing this particular issue of the magazine. As well as my own team of copyeditors, a prominent neurophysiologist

had collaborated on the issue and meticulously
checked every article and illustration. The authors
had also approved the final edited copy of their own
articles.

Here we were after months of work, at the very
last moment, ready to roll. Any delay, especially
stopping the press run, would cost a lot of time and
money. Besides, one of the world's foremost experts
on brain scans had supplied the illustration and
its accompanying labels. They couldn't be wrong,
could they, I asked myself.

Despite that and despite wanting to get the magazine out on time, I trusted my intuition and ordered
the job to be pulled off the press. Back home, after
several hours of phoning around, I finally reached
the brain scan specialist. Fortunately he had his cell
phone on. It was a Saturday and he was playing
golf.

I explained the situation to him, and he suggested
I call his chief assistant and set up a three-way telephone connection. The other fellow happened to
be in the office that day. When he joined our conversation and loaded up the computer file showing
the original of the illustration they had supplied
for the magazine, he was shocked to discover that
it had been mislabeled from the start. So not only
were two of the colors too similar looking, worse
yet, they were identifying the wrong types of tissue
altogether! Such a fundamental error could have
undermined the entire issue's credibility – another
lesson for me in the value of minding one's gut.

The nose knows

Gut intuition or instinct is a perfect term. Instinct means an impulse, thought, or behavior that results not from conscious reasoning but from deep within our nature or being. It describes anything we know or feel intuitively, without evidence. Often, of course, we do rely on our intuition, like whether to trust people we meet. But here I'm referring to even more subtle instances of intuition.

These fleeting moments of insight, doubt, or unease, while transitory and mental, are so real that they can hit us palpably in our physical senses. I feel these gut reactions or warnings as a slight twinge, twisting, or queasiness in my stomach. Some people feel an itch or tickle in their nose, which explains another bodily expression for this phenomenon, "the nose knows." Still others might experience a second of slight dizziness or blurriness, as if a synapse in the brain had misfired, like a car's spark plug missing a beat and warning of trouble ahead.

I can't emphasize enough the value of developing the confidence to heed and, more importantly, respond to intuitive flashes. Numerous times I've found in my own work that pursuing these fleeting warnings or clues, despite my inclinations to avoid them and move on, has led me to uncover key information about a subject, a serious error, or a whole new avenue of investigation.

Follow up on anything odd or puzzling.

In meetings and interviews, for example, get into the habit of following up on inconsistencies or anything slightly puzzling that slips out during the course of discussion. If someone says something that you don't quite understand or that seems anomalous to everything else said thus far, instead of letting it pass, head exactly in that direction.

You can say simply, "Sorry, could you say that again?" or "I didn't quite understand that; could you please explain it to me?" If you can't immediately follow up on your gut reaction, jot down a note so that you remember to return to it before leaving the meeting or at some opportune time later.

Pursuing a seemingly inconsequential twist often leads to the most revealing line of inquiry. Sometimes it exposes a sensitive or critical issue that underlies what, until then, had been forgotten or purposely avoided, but was in fact essential. Perhaps no one is ready yet to face up to the real issue or to state it directly. But when you notice a slight inconsistency or something questionable, and then return to it appropriately – gently or directly – you may end up helping your associates, boss, client, or friend to resolve and communicate a burning issue.

Respond appropriately to each situation.

Pursuing a seemingly inconsequential twist often leads to the most revealing line of inquiry.

Following up things that are slightly askew often leads me to clarify and then solve – or at least communicate – an issue that, until then, had been so difficult for an individual or company to deal with and explain that, while fundamental, was ignored. One time, for example, when I encountered some confusion after asking a client how one of their particular products was actually used, I helped them face the fact that they needed to do some basic market research.

Almost without exception, my clients are relieved when such issues are finally brought out into the open and made lucid. When a veil of ignorance and uncertainty is lifted, everyone reaches new levels of understanding.

They find unexpected clarity and a sense of purpose that allows them to move forward, mobilize resources, and exceed their expectations.

Grab momentary ideas

Gut intuitions don't just give warnings; they also reveal innovative ideas and lead to breakthroughs. When I'm receiving a first briefing on a new project, I frequently experience a spontaneous brainstorm where a creative idea such as an advertising slogan or brand name suddenly pops into mind. The freshness of the moment stimulates a rush of creativity.

Capture the freshness of the moment.

As I noted in the first chapter, I've learned to hold back from divulging these ideas on the spot. Further investigation and consideration might reveal more appropriate solutions or raise questions about the initial thought. I've also learned that people typically give more value to things that appear to be the result of long, painstaking labor rather than direct insight.

Which reminds me of an amusing story I once heard about showmanship. Shortly after graduating from university, I was visiting Rome and in a restaurant met a businessman who offered me a ride to Florence. On the way we stopped for lunch in Pisa and he told me about his business. He had invented a revolutionary technology for cleaning clogged, corroded oil pipelines. But his system worked so fast and easily that he found it difficult to charge the high fee companies had been used to paying for this critical, formerly laborious maintenance service.

So instead of performing the service as quickly as he actually could, he would hire a team of people, like extras in a film, and post them along the pipeline route, armed with flares and walkie-talkies. They fired their flares and consulted each other frequently over the closed communication system for several hours before and after the actual work, which took only minutes. In effect, he staged a theatrical extravaganza to dramatize his otherwise speedy technical performance and hence justify his high fee. Everyone was satisfied.

I'm not advocating such theatrics. Spontaneous solutions, however, do need to be considered and presented with greater elaboration. And not so long after I heard that story, I learned in my own work to withhold any breakthrough ideas I come up with, allowing further time and deliberation to take their course.

Despite this caveat, don't ignore any sudden or "crazy" ideas about your work. Jot them down no matter how off-key or silly they seem at first. No harm is done by recording something in your notebook. No one need see them until you're sure they're right – another reason for allowing time to pass. But take advantage of every moment of life and the rich resources of your marvelous mind's ability to see beyond its five senses.

Jot down your ideas, even "crazy" ones.

Break habits of denial

Having failed often enough myself to mind – to perceive and follow up on – a momentary hunch that something was wrong (or that something was right), I've asked myself, Why? Why do I and most everyone else not fully trust our power of intuition, the peripheral vision of our minds? In my experience, it's because of one of the following five reasons. All are habitual forms of denial and should be cast aside.

The first reason is that we tend to underrate the importance or priority of our gut feelings and other little warnings. Perhaps they seem too small or insignificant in contrast to the big, tough issues and crises that consume our time and attention. The staffs of many businesses and other organizations find themselves dealing with one crisis after another. Committees often devour much of our time. Meetings, panics, and tight deadlines waylay our attention and keep us from working more methodically and responding to subtle stimuli.

As a result, like at a hospital emergency ward, we've consciously or unconsciously established a triage system. When problems emerge, we identify and deal first with the most urgent priority cases, leaving seemingly minor ones sitting around for hours until they're forgotten or disappear, or it's too late.

Meetings, panics, and tight deadlines waylay our attention and keep us from working more methodically and responding to subtle stimuli.

This system breaks down when the minor cases turn out to have been masking serious problems or major opportunities. By then it's usually too late to do anything about them. They're "dead, dying, or permanently injured," to complete the analogy. The reverse, of course, is also true: the triage system fails when we avoid tackling major problems or priorities and instead fritter away our time, occupying ourselves with trivial matters. Either way – in avoiding serious issues or underrating subtle cues – we're misjudging reality.

Respond to serious issues and subtle cues.

A second reason we fail to respond to twinges of doubt is that we're embarrassed to reveal our ignorance. Let's say you're meeting with your boss and she's setting out a new project. Something she says in passing doesn't quite make sense. Maybe you feel it's something you should already understand; after all, no one else at the meeting is raising any questions. So if you're the only one on your team who doesn't seem to get it, you fear you'll look bad if you bring it up. You'll look stupid.

Whenever I've followed up on such doubts instead of hiding from them out of embarrassment, I've usually found that others shared my misgivings or confusion and were glad I raised the issue. And biggest surprise of all, the leader is often the most grateful, perhaps even admitting that this was something he or she wasn't certain of or had failed to see.

The third reason we miss little mistakes or gaps is that we assume they must already have been checked out or resolved or, in the case of creative ideas, that someone must already have come up with that one; it's too obvious. For example, someone must have confirmed a particular fact or statistic or it wouldn't be in a draft, certainly not at an advanced stage of the work, near the end. Or an illustration must be accurate or it wouldn't have been supplied by experts in the first place, just like my story about the brain scan at the beginning of this chapter.

In short, we want to believe in things. If we express doubt, we're seen as pessimists and naysayers. In this tough, competitive world we're supposed to act like optimists, not doubters. Doubters are losers, right?

But cynicism and realism are not the same things. Mistakes do happen. Murphy's Law describes an actual phenomenon: often enough, things that can go wrong do so. Anticipating problems and catching a whiff of something possibly wrong doesn't make you a cynic, but a realist and a good manager. Of course, you don't have to act out of fear and paranoia. Simply be aware and respond appropriately.

The fourth reason mistakes are missed or seemingly unimportant items are disregarded is that we often avoid taking responsibility. If you bring up a question in a meeting, for example, you'll probably be designated as the person to deal with it. Better to forget it and not add further work to your already hectic and stressful life, or so you might tell yourself. After all, you can't be responsible for everything, can you? For example, even though you might think about it and feel a twinge of moral obligation, you don't pick up every piece of garbage you walk by or help out every beggar you pass.

No, of course not, and there's no reason to feel guilty about it either. But in those domains that do define our lives, at home or at work, when everyone avoids responsibility, inaction turns into group ethic. A veil of silence and ignorance descends, obscuring reality, denigrating performance, and diminishing self-respect. Over time, little problems build up, like molten lava ready to erupt.

Avoiding responsibility also happens at a more subtle level – simple laziness, the fifth reason we ignore our gut feelings. Laziness is not altogether bad. It's not necessary to live a constantly active life for it to be fulfilling. Problems arise, though, when we don't do what needs being done and what, deep in our heart, we truly want to do. A little laziness is healthy; chronic laziness is avoiding life itself.

Take on responsibilities; ward off chronic laziness.

Working the core of being

Instead of avoiding life, we can choose to embrace it and take pride in a job well done and in being open and courageous in our work. Work is part of life. I'll repeat that: *work is part of life.*

I've often wondered why people work at something if they don't really care about it. I know, of course, that this attitude reflects considerable luxury, and that hundreds of millions of people all over the world must work in unpleasant and unhealthy circumstances to survive and barely support their families. Everyone needs to earn a living, and relatively few people have much choice about what they can do.

I realize as well that I've been fortunate throughout most of my life to do work I actually care about and that challenges and intrigues me. Regardless, I think the world would be a healthier place if more people genuinely valued what they work at, whether it's cleaning out sewers or teaching children in school. Ideally, every task ought to be worthwhile, or it shouldn't be done.

Enjoy work; it's your life.

Trusting your gut instinct, your intuition, helps to bring life home into the moment.

Certainly in the developed world most people have more choices in what they do, and yet many of us still tend to separate our lives emotionally from our work, as if five or six days a week we cease living for eight hours. Again, I recognize that I live differently from most people in that I've nearly always worked independently, and so the demarcation between work and the rest of my life is blurred.

Nevertheless, all life is work, and all work is life. Our hearts and souls continue to tick regardless of where we are or what we're doing. In the purest sense, wherever you are is your home. Home is what exists in the moment, in the present, in the now. And trusting your gut instinct, your intuition, helps to bring life home into the moment.

Like many idiomatic phrases, the words *gut instinct* contain much native wisdom. In a physical sense, the gut is literally your center of gravity, the base of your power. Most martial arts systems – whether Western-style wrestling or Eastern-style self-defense – teach practitioners to draw strength and power by centering themselves in their abdomen. The gut is the core of your physical being.

It's also the core of your psychic or inner being. Hence many meditation systems teach people to focus on breathing from the lower abdomen. Moving away from the customary focus on your head leads you toward sensing and relating to things more deeply and directly, using your power of intuition.

Focus on your full being, not just your head.

Particularly in the West, we think that our minds reside strictly in our brains. All thoughts and perceptions come from the brain, or so our brain tells us. But this makes for a rather restricted view of our mental capacity. In fact, your mental being is part and parcel of your entire being and everything around you. You sense things without your brain instructing you to do so. And you know things without your brain having to inform you.

By centering yourself more deeply in your gut, you can tune in more sensitively to your greater being, a being that perceives and knows things instinctively and immediately. Not that there's anything wrong with thinking actively and using your brain's intellect. The brain is a wonderful organ. But your ability to know things need not be restricted to intellectual constructions alone. Minding your gut opens up your deeper powers and your connection to your surroundings.

So learn to hear and heed those little twinges of doubt or uncertainty and those sudden creative, inspirational flashes. They're real.

YOUR STORY

List one to three instances when you realized later
you had failed to follow up on a gut reaction to
something you saw, heard, or were working on. Did
your hesitation have any repercussions? Then list
one to three instances where you did pay attention
to your intuition. How did it pay off? Send your lists
to www.WordsBecomeYou.com. And share the
website and this book with friends and coworkers.

4

Simplify to One

To communicate effectively, synthesize your information and identify one simple unifying theme or mission. Simplicity isn't simplistic, however, but rich in meaning and nuance.

HOW AMAZING THAT, despite life's infinite complexity, our minds appear to think in coherent blocks of thoughts and ideas, and we speak using intelligible clumps of words and sentences. Our concepts and words have significance for us and convey meaning to other people; in turn, other people speak to us. We communicate.

Time and space also appear to make sense. One moment seems to follow another, time proceeds along an ostensibly linear path, and the world looks familiar from one day to the next.

In reality – a reality made evident by modern physics but long familiar in metaphysics – the world turns out to be utterly unfixed. Nothing remains the same from one instant to the next, even if we perceive consistency. Atoms, molecules, and all matter exist in a state of constant flux.

Stranger yet, at the subatomic level, past, present, and future get all mixed up, requiring a number of extra dimensions to make sense of reality. Even more weird, subatomic particles separated by vast distances act in concert, defying our conventional concepts of linear time and space. The deeper science looks, the more mysterious everything turns out to be. Neither reality nor our ideas about it remain certain. Change, as the saying goes, is the only constant.

We, too, change constantly despite picturing ourselves as having a singular and fixed self-identity. Like constellations in space filled with stars, our minds are packed with billions of nerve cells. The cells fire off to one another in untold numbers of connections, creating ever-changing networks of meaning and coherence.

Similar to space, though, our minds contain far more emptiness than solid matter. If we ponder deeply into our individuality, what we find is not a singular, fixed identity, but something more infinite and open-ended, something far more beautiful and interconnected with all the other constellations. As with individual particles, our consciousness and imagination defy the limits of time and space, connecting with past, present, and future and with individuals beyond our immediate reach. We're like droplets of water in the ocean, distinct but at the same time part of a collective sea, the waves of time and space rolling through again and again.

Within this endlessly churning sea of life, however, we each have individual identities. Scientists and philosophers have long struggled to figure out how a sense of self is constructed within the mind. Today, while many scientists seek a grand unifying theory that explains all physical reality, others strive to explain human consciousness.

I doubt that either puzzle will ever be solved because the act of observation itself raises a fundamental paradox: confined within the limits of the physical universe, we cannot completely explain that universe. Nor by using our own minds can we totally define ourselves. No single, describable truth exists, for even if there were one truth, by definition it could not be delineated by words. Words are limiting; truth is not.

Nevertheless, just as we each have a singular identity despite life's constant flux, so too can we create coherent unifying ideas or themes to address the complex tasks we undertake and the ideas we wish to communicate. Not only can we do this; it's how we function normally.

By using our innate power to synthesize complicated matter into singular ideas, we're able to connect with people and work effectively. By boiling ideas down into one simple overall message, we help others to follow along with what we say or do. Singular ideas capture attention and bring people together.

Use singular themes to communicate effectively.

MY STORY

Expressing community

Each time I approach a new assignment, I feel overwhelmed by the subject's complexity. How can I as an outsider pull everything together and make the subject coherent for others? Fortunately, I've learned that I can, and so can you.

For over a decade, I edited and produced what became an internationally respected journal on auto accidents and injuries. The initial assignment called for something less ambitious.

One of the largest casualty insurers in North America – a public corporation that held the monopoly in its jurisdiction on motor vehicle liability insurance – wanted to improve its credibility with the medical and legal communities. Lawyers and health practitioners directly influence the settlement of personal injury cases through their relations with the injured parties. People look to their lawyers,

doctors, and other health providers for guidance on
how to recover and how to get compensation for
their losses. Generally speaking, the longer a case
remains open, the more costly it is to settle. Hence,
my client wanted good relations with lawyers and
doctors in order to control escalating costs.

Unfortunately, the medical and health professions mistrusted the insurance corporation even
more than they mistrusted each other. Although
the system operated as a monopoly, supposedly for
the public good, it still functioned according to the
fault principle: to get compensation for their losses,
injured people had to sue the responsible party.

In actual fact, you had to fight your own insurance company, since the same company you bought
your insurance from by law had to represent not
you, but the other party, the alleged wrongdoer. In
other words, your insurance covered not your own
loss but the losses that you might cause to others.
This made for lots of litigation, with huge expenses
resulting from each side's obtaining often conflict-
ing medical and other evidence.

The highly adversarial environment was ex-
acerbated by the fact that injured people had to
confront an insurance company that was not only
their own insurer but also a government body. Few
came out a winner, and certainly not the genuinely
injured people. Typically they had to wait years for
their final settlement, all the time focusing on their
unsettled losses, often delaying their recovery by not
getting on with their lives.

How in this unhappy environment could the
insurance corporation issue any kind of communication that would improve its credibility? After
considering the situation for a couple of months

and interviewing people in the target audience, I came back with straightforward advice: "You want to improve your credibility? Simple. Do something credible."

I recommended that the corporation fund a journal that would address the topic of injury in a direct, substantive manner, not shirking as most corporate or government propaganda does from controversy. As well, I suggested that the target audience itself be enlisted to write the articles. The publication would thus serve as a genuine medium of communication among all parties.

Even more fundamentally, the journal would treat the subject holistically. Injury would be seen not just as recovering from physical hurt, but also in terms of the entire system's requiring a form of healing. The journal would deal with everything from driver behavior, policing, transportation planning, vehicle and roadway engineering, insurance, and the justice system to emergency response, trauma care, and physical, emotional, and spiritual rehabilitation. All aspects together formed a whole picture. And the single theme, the synthesis, that tied them all together was *healing* – the recovery of health and wholeness.

As it turned out, each issue of the journal also addressed a single unifying topic, such as brain injury, alternative dispute resolution, transportation safety, and trauma care. The subjects proved limitless since transportation and its impacts permeate society. By keeping the focus on recovery – on healing – and by editing the articles written by experts in each field so that professionals in other areas could readily understand them, the journal raised the dialogue above the level of bickering and mistrust.

The magazine operated with one purpose only: to prevent and reduce unnecessary human misery. This was a value which everyone could endorse, expressing a single community of interest. As it turned out, the magazine actually helped to prevent deaths and injuries and to improve the overall environment for recovery, all under the umbrella of one simple, encompassing theme.

Give your audience a hand

While they should never become fixed and precious, single ideas make sense out of complexity. Without perspective, subjects can't be clearly communicated. Think of the times you've left a lecture or a movie and wondered what it was all about. Perhaps it seemed clear while you were reading, hearing, or watching whatever it was, but later you can't remember much about the experience. The memory fades into obscurity.

There's nothing wrong with complexity. And there's no rule that everything should make absolutely clear sense. When you want to communicate effectively, however, try to synthesize your information and find a single theme, image, name, slogan, insight, or other device.

The same principle applies to completing any complex task. You are more likely to succeed if you synthesize the work into one guiding mission, goal, or focus. Devices like this give people a handle to hold onto. Think of it also like a lens or focus through which people can see the detail more clearly. Synthesizing means boiling down, distilling, drawing together, and coherently expressing the essence of something.

Why is this necessary? Because nearly everyone's life these days is so hectic, so filled with information, so fast paced, you can't expect people to hear or see – let alone

understand and remember – your particular message or
mission when it's lost in the maze of competing stuff.
But a single hook or unifying idea can capture people's
attention, focus their concentration, and help them form
a longer-lasting impression and understanding. This is as
true for a speech given to a local club as it is for a film,
a novel, or an advertising campaign. Effective, singular
themes help people understand and relate to otherwise
intricate information.

The trick is that the single theme or idea should be
cogent, powerful, and memorable. It should also reflect
if not actually express and embody the work's essential
purpose. In doing so the theme provides more than an
overall idea: it gives you a tool to organize your material.
Like the musical theme in a symphony that repeats again
and again but in various forms to express the mood of
each section and tie the whole piece together, your central
idea can be repeated, developed, and modulated over the
course of your work. A solid theme helps you to create
meaning and order for both yourself and others.

Develop a theme that relates to your purpose.

---

*Effective, singular themes help people
understand and relate to otherwise
intricate information.*

But remember, your theme or organizing idea should
be true.

Hold on a second! Didn't I just say that no single idea
can be true? Yes, strictly speaking, no single idea can be
absolutely true, and we make a big mistake when we think
so. But symbolically – and all words and communication

are, after all, symbolic in that they represent thoughts or things but are not the things themselves – single ideas can reflect reality if they're genuine. Language communicates most effectively when it conveys real meaning. Genuine ideas are borne from honest introspection, not from self-deception or fabrication.

Unity and complexity are one

Given the complexity of most everything these days, how can cogent, single ideas be synthesized and expressed? This dilemma arises most particularly when you find yourself so close to a subject that, so to speak, "you can't see the forest for the trees." Because you're involved personally and intensely in an issue or subject, often all you can make out is its complexity. You get bogged down and lost in the detail. How can it be reduced to one essential concept when each aspect seems to complicate if not contradict another?

Contradictions and complications inevitably arise when you closely examine any subject, just as they inevitably arise in the complex relations among people. Don't get carried away by complexity.

And don't worry about purity either. Finding the right single concept or idea should not be confused with purity. Nothing is pure to the nth degree. We want purity with all our hearts, but the more we search for it, the more we grow frustrated or, worse yet, the more likely we are to be fooled by charlatans proclaiming that they alone have the one and only answer.

The lack of purity does not, however, mean that ideas cannot be simplified or expressed plainly. Any subject no matter how complex can be synthesized. That is the power you and I all possess: the mind naturally seeks order and clarity. By trusting this inherent faculty, you develop a knack for identifying the commonalities as well as the contrasts in the many aspects of a given subject. Through this process, you will more easily perceive a single concept that unites them all. The contradictions and complications will remain, but so will the unity.

Identify your subject's contrasts and commonalities.

Herein lies a key to reducing things to one: realizing that unity and complexity are not mutually exclusive. They're opposite sides of the same coin.

Look at the sky, for example. Say that today the sky above you in Vancouver is cloudy. You're speaking to a friend in New York who asks about the weather. You answer, "It's cloudy today." That's true, isn't it? In fact, the sky is filled not only with thousands of clouds of different sizes and shapes, but billions upon billions of the ionized water molecules that form clouds. Yes, it's cloudy.

At least it looks cloudy from where you are. Up closer you might fixate on the separate puffs; closer yet, on the molecules. Your perspective changes what you see and how you express it. But remember, when you communicate you're speaking to people whose perspective differs from your own. You may be looking deep into the clouds with a telescope or at molecules with a microscope, but everyone else is wondering what kind of clothes to wear today.

Know that unity and complexity go hand in hand.

And here lies the even deeper key to expressing a singular idea: if you want to communicate effectively, realize how to convey your idea not merely in your own frame of reference, but also in that of your audience. Uncover where your perceptions, emotions, worries, and hopes meet those of the people you wish to reach out to. You'll be surprised to find that they meet as one, far more often than not. Realize as well that, just like subatomic particles, in the great scheme of things people are not truly separate. Find the commonality between you and others, and express it.

Inspiring simplicity

Without perhaps realizing it, in expressing yourself you're constantly using singular notions and ideas held in common with others. Communication and commonality come naturally because they are the natural state of being. Suddenly, however, when we set out consciously to talk about a topic we're close to, we start to worry and get frustrated by all the detail. How can we possibly simplify or synthesize this mass of information, we ask ourselves. How can we connect to people who don't know the subject as well as we do?

When you arrive at this point of frustration, take it as a signal to pull away from your research and analysis. Stop struggling to find a way to synthesize your material or define a mission clearly. Instead, watch those clouds, go out for a walk or run, sit and meditate, or do whatever it is you do to take a break. This is where "trusting nothing" again proves useful. Having done your investigation, having examined all the detail, and also having considered the commonalities, give your mind the time and space it needs to perceive – suddenly or gradually – the single idea that brings it all together.

Trust your mind's facility for synthesis.

Wait a moment, are things really that simple? Isn't it naive to think that complex topics or issues can be reduced to just one idea or one theme?

This troubled me, too. I used to worry that I tended to simplify things too much. But I came to see the difference between simple and simplistic. *Simple* means to see, express, or deal with things in a straightforward manner, unencumbered by detail. *Simplistic* means to oversimplify or ignore all the detail. I'm not advising that you ignore anything, but that you express things more clearly using lucid and straightforward organizing concepts.

Of course, sometimes a topic is so complicated it seems impossible to express it using one concept alone. Even in such cases, however, you can still provide your readers or audience with a coherent, unified context within which they can approach the subject's intricacies without getting lost in the detail. By establishing a clear focus for a subject, you help people understand and cope with its complexities rather than becoming further confused and frustrated by them.

Give focus and clarity even to complexity.

Again, it's important to realize that simplicity, singularity, and commonality are compatible with complexity, diversity, and multiplicity. When you say the sky is cloudy, you're not denying that it's also made up of an ever-changing myriad of shapes and particles. You're just helping people get a grasp of the condition – and pick the right clothes to wear.

Simplicity, singularity, and commonality are compatible with complexity, diversity, and multiplicity.

Similarly, in grasping that we're all connected and interdependent, you're not denying your own unique individuality or anyone else's. The two realities exist as one. You and others – all of us – are linked in one reality. Without others to be in relationship with, no singular self could exist. Indeed, in realizing the interdependence of life we also acknowledge the individual responsibility we each have, since everything we do affects everything else.

Communication does not differ from living. If you get caught up in the vast complexity of your life, you stop functioning. And people do stop functioning when they feel overwhelmed. They fall into depression and stay in bed – or, more commonly these days, take pills to cope with their problems.

When you're functioning normally, you keep doing things in the face of reality's vast and uncompromising complexity and its infinite contradictions. You may call it an act of faith if you wish, but each day you're alive you work and create even though in the next moment you may not be alive. Nothing is permanent, and yet you continue to manifest yourself fluently, moment by moment.

If you have faith in yourself and relate to your audience, you will find a simple and clear way to express things meaningfully to others.

Communication transpires similarly, moment by moment. Despite the confusion you may feel surrounding a topic, if you have faith in yourself and relate to your audience, you will find a simple and clear way to express things meaningfully to others. The idea is there already; you only need look within yourself to reveal it.

The chief creative director at one of the major New York–based international advertising agencies once described this process as "inspired simplicity." The inspired part is essential. To merely simplify a topic for the sake of simplification will get you nowhere. The single idea must arise from reality. After struggling through detail, simplicity feels like a breath of fresh air taken in after crawling through a tight and stuffy cavern. Inspiration comes from the depth of your heart and soul.

Admittedly, sometimes it doesn't come: no single idea emerges. Don't give up hope. Sometimes it isn't possible to boil everything down to one single theme or concept. Maybe you can only reduce a subject to two or three principal ideas. That's okay. Focusing on one idea isn't virtuous or the only truth; it's just a way to make a subject more lucid.

If you can't get to one, boil things down to two or three.

So don't feel compelled to discover only one idea. Even more important, don't allow yourself to be taken in by your own singular ideas or those of others. Singular ideas are useful tools. They're not gods.

Unfortunately, throughout history, dictators and other demagogues have used single ideas to mesmerize people into doing horrible things in the name of "truth." Driven by their madness and thirst for power, demagogues turn single ideas into rigid ideologies, leading masses of people to believe their mission is true and all others are false and must be destroyed. God is on their side; no one else's.

Think of the Third Reich built on lies and skillful propaganda. Fortunately the Third Reich did not last its promised 1000 years, for lies don't usually seem to survive the test of time. People eventually awaken to the inherent complexity of life and dismiss rigid ideologies. Sadly, a great deal of havoc and tragedy is wreaked in the meantime.

Remember that ideas are useful, not absolute.

Don't get stuck in your own unifying ideas either. Never forget that, like life itself, ideas and concepts exist in a state of constant flux. To take them as unchanging, fixed, truths breaks down communication and violates the harmony and beauty of life. Communication is a living, breathing, endless human connection.

YOUR STORY

Explain in one paragraph a complex issue you've recently dealt with or written about, or one you're currently facing. Now simplify everything into one single concept: describe in one concluding sentence the essential idea or synthesis underlying the whole issue. If you like, rewrite the paragraph bringing your synthesis closer to the beginning. Send your composition to www.WordsBecomeYou.com.

5

Do Reinvent the Wheel

No matter how often you've done the identical project, addressed the same topic, or reasoned with the same person, treat each occasion in life as new and fresh. Creativity keeps your spirit alive.

YOU'RE SITTING AT YOUR DESK struggling to figure out how to tell a longtime supplier that you're switching to a different manufacturer. You've had a long and mutually rewarding relationship with the company. Its managers have extended themselves to help you out in difficult circumstances, shifting their production schedule and delivering items to you faster than usual. Now you have to tell them that you're ending the relationship because your company's found a cheaper supplier. What to say?

A coworker passes by and hearing your dilemma says, "What's the big deal? We've canceled suppliers before. Just use one of our old letters. Don't reinvent the wheel."

Or this scenario: You're working with a team to develop a new model of washer-dryer that your company plans to distribute to markets across the continent. You have decades of past consumer research and a wealth of previous experience to draw on for reference. Your company has long commanded a leading market share.

But market demographics have changed, and people have different expectations for appliances. You propose taking a totally new approach to product planning and design. But the rest of your team thinks you're making unnecessary work for everyone. "Let's just get on with it," they say. "We already have a method that's worked for years. Don't reinvent the wheel."

And then there's government. Say you've worked in the same department for fifteen years, handling company registrations and complaints about alleged corporate wrongdoings. You've heard every kind of problem and every sort of explanation. One day you get a letter from a distraught mother who feels she was seriously misled by a store's advertising of a particular toy's safety features.

Life is an adventure, and creativity keeps the spirit alive. Besides, it's the only way to do a job right.

It's hardly the first time you've heard something like this, and you have standard form letters to send to both the parent and the store. Yet, that night, you keep wondering if you shouldn't look further into this particular complaint. It's left you with a hollow feeling in the pit of your stomach: maybe something potentially serious really happened. But why bother to do anything out of the routine? You'd just be creating more work for yourself. And it probably wouldn't do any good anyway. Don't reinvent the wheel, you tell yourself.

Doing things differently can definitely be a nuisance. Creativity takes extra time and extra effort, or so it seems.

The "tried and true" looks easier and safer. I often feel this way myself, hesitant to try something new or too lazy to put out the extra effort. But if I felt that way a lot of the time, I'd seriously have to ask myself, Why bother living at all? The answer: life is an adventure, and creativity keeps the spirit alive. Besides, it's the only way to do a job right.

MY STORY

Surprising again and again

One of the most satisfying projects I ever had, as described in the previous chapter, was editing and publishing some 50 issues of an international journal on roadway crashes and injuries. The journal covered a great array of topics all united by the theme of healing. Producing each issue took a huge amount of work; I could have tired of the routine, and sometimes I did.

Motivated to retain the contract, however, as well as feeling altruistic about the subject, I established a practice of constant renewal. I decided that each new issue should surprise readers by addressing an unusual topic or treating a subject strikingly different from what would ordinarily be expected from a government-sponsored publication. Issue themes ranged from multicultural concepts of healing to more philosophical questions such as the nature of truth. For the latter issue, for example, the topics included witness credibility, judging the legitimacy of claims, the accuracy and influence of news reporting, and how much of the truth about their condition should be revealed to severely injured people.

The strategy of constant renewal – of reinventing the wheel for each new issue – contributed to the magazine's growing success and recognition. Although it started as a journal aimed at a few thousand doctors and lawyers in one jurisdiction, it ended up being read by over 75,000 diverse professionals in nearly forty countries.

I also strived to make each issue surpass the previous one stylistically, in content, or in concept. Major commercial magazines don't operate this way; they offer a consistent product from day one in order to appeal to a precise demographic readership and satisfy their advertisers. As a subsidized, special interest magazine, we could afford to do things differently. My editorial staff and I enjoyed the luxury of not having to rely on ads and paid subscriptions. But we still had to produce something of value for our readers.

We adopted a policy of reinvention not simply to be different, but because it accurately represented the reality that crashes and injuries result from diverse factors and affect a broad swath of society.

The ideas that generated each new issue and appealed freshly to the readership arose from our growing facility to look directly into the subject matter and respond appropriately. Creativity arises from caring about life – and taking action.

Blinded by efficiency

The creative force may seem irrelevant to much of your daily work. Why waste time, for example, when things are already thoroughly understood and procedures long established? Forms, formulas, and boilerplates certainly have reasonable applications. A law firm, for example, produces similar types of contracts and other legal documents again and again. It makes little sense to redraft paragraphs that are used repeatedly. Instead, they can be systematically organized and pulled together to suit each particular situation.

Similarly, whether you're a bureaucrat in a large government department or a senior assistant to the CEO of a major corporation, the economies of scale dictate using forms and form letters when dealing with mass numbers of inquiries and continual correspondence. It seems sensible and efficient to automate communication when you must respond to hundreds of messages day after day, week after week.

At the same time, we can all remember receiving personally addressed letters that somewhere midway through the document addressed us by the wrong name or alluded to a situation without any relevance to our own. You may have laughed it off or, more likely, crumpled up the letter and tossed into the wastepaper basket. The automated system had failed.

Direct marketing and computerization have grown more sophisticated and simple breakdowns occur less frequently. Maybe the system works too perfectly. Nowadays our private affairs and personal habits can readily be recorded, evaluated, and utilized to a precise and somewhat insidious degree for the purposes of marketing and advertising. Every single purchase you make at a cashier, every Web site you log onto, every bank transaction you make, and every telephone call you place can potentially be recorded and tabulated not only for the sake of evaluating mass markets but also for following up with you individually.

The systematization pervasive in our culture not only has an enormous impact on our privacy, the communication derived from these systems also lacks a truly personal touch. No matter how sophisticated the formula, direct marketing and similar mass communications come across as obsequious and fake. Most people can smell the depersonalized, insincere tone. Nevertheless, such campaigns must provide an adequate return on investment or direct marketing wouldn't be a multibillion-dollar industry.

But that's the industry. What about applying systems to your own everyday work? Here, too, depersonalization spells trouble. Depending on boilerplates and form responses can lead to miscommunication – and serious errors.

Professional consultants, for example, working under pressure to build up chargeable hours and increase their efficiency, naturally slip into the habit of using standardized documents and other systems. Operating under this pressure, putting in many hours of overtime, they can easily misinterpret a particular situation, causing minor embarrassments like using the wrong name, or major and costly mistakes like giving damaging advice. Potential liability works against committing such mistakes. But the fear of liability also engenders ever more complex procedures and confusing contractual language employed for self-protection rather than communication.

Many professionals and businesspeople might consider it problematic if not outright dangerous to respond freshly to each situation as it arises rather than rely on a formulated response. Why put yourself on the line if a problem has already been solved? Why take chances? Why reinvent the wheel?

Tradition and change coexist

Unfortunately, this kind of thinking has created vast amounts of standardized, often confusing communication and legions of bureaucracies operating with labyrinthine procedures. When individuals and organizations grow to rely solely on what's been done before, the past piles up like old clothes. No longer worn, they crowd your closet so that you can't find what you want to wear – a situation familiar to me – let alone come up with something new and inventive.

A self-righteous ethic accumulates along with all this detritus. Anyone who questions the way things have been done before is judged as inefficient or, worse, as a threat to the status quo. People and organizations develop a vested interest in doing things the same way partly out of emotional or ideological attachment, but more so because of money. The keepers of tradition get paid doing the same things over and over again. Change threatens their status and livelihood.

The two forces of tradition and creativity nourish each other in a dynamic process of reinvention.

I've done a number of projects for universities. Everything worked fine when I produced a communication piece and left it at that. But once when I took on a temporary assignment, filling a role within the institution, I came up against a wall. Not only was I unfamiliar with the standard ways of doing things and accepted modes of behavior, I also acted undiplomatically, trying to reinvent the wheel too aggressively. And so I failed. Even "liberal" institutions are imbedded in traditions, and I didn't know how to fit it.

Traditions in themselves are not a bad thing. They provide us with a storehouse of experience, wisdom, and helpful guidelines. Traditions go haywire, however, when they're employed to block open-mindedness and new vision. Traditions are a foundation, not a "be all and end all."

More fundamentally, there's no reason that tradition and change cannot coexist. People can draw on their traditions while also expanding their horizons. In fact, the two forces of tradition and creativity nourish each other in a dynamic process of reinvention. Using history to reflect on new situations and building on past experience are useful creative strategies as long as you also maintain an open mind. But traditionalists often try to block all change and revolutionaries aim to destroy all tradition.

Draw on tradition but stay open to change.

Ideology is a swamp in which life sinks into ossification and decay.

Problems arise when people get stuck in ideology, traditional or revolutionary. Ideology is a swamp in which life sinks into ossification and decay. Ideologues always believe they are absolutely right and everyone else is absolutely wrong, whether fighting to preserve their god or their politics – or, more troubling, the two combined. Ideology may work for a while, but eventually it breaks down.

Efficiency for efficiency's sake is also an insidious form of ideology. Ostensibly, when people dismiss a new idea or ridicule a fresh approach to an issue, and then say, Don't reinvent the wheel, they're encouraging you to work efficiently. Don't waste your time, they seem to be advising. In actual fact, they're squelching creativity.

Take the wheel, itself, as a prime example – specifically, the modern world's use of the wheel combined with the internal combustion engine. Society got hooked on this technology starting at the end of the nineteenth century. It worked. It turned energy into movement more efficiently than the steam engine. Unfortunately, the technology has also produced earth-killing pollution and made the world dependent on limited resources found predominantly in a region of the world that specializes in trouble.

This is a "wheel" that should have been reinvented early on. But a vast industrial complex grew up around motor vehicles, including not just the petroleum and automobile manufacturing industries, but also steel, rubber, plastic, asphalt, and concrete manufacturers; the mass media and advertising industries; unions; transportation engineers; bus companies; truckers; auto clubs; litigation lawyers; and insurance companies – all with deep-rooted, vested interests that favor a gas-driven automobile infrastructure over more efficient alternative transportation modes and technologies.

Reinventing the forever new

So what do all these "wheels" have to do with communication? In short, everything.

Communication travels via a moving vehicle, shifting position and changing shape every instant. We hear and speak to people now, in the present, not in the past or the future. To the extent that we're stuck in the past or the future, we don't hear accurately and we don't speak authentically. Genuine communication as with doing any kind of task requires presence of mind. Anything that impedes our being present – including compulsive fear, doubt, anger, or excessive thinking – gets in the way.

Prejudice and preconception are two particular mental hang-ups that block our facility to hear others, inhibiting our ability to respond creatively and appropriately to the circumstances. There's nothing wrong per se with personal taste. But when we become possessed by biases and prejudgments, the resulting fixed positions narrow our minds. Narrow-mindedness shrinks the scope of our sensory perception and atrophies our otherwise natural capacity to interact and respond creatively. In other words, we shut down.

Which means communication shuts down, because openness lies at the root of fluent communication. Openness implies newness. Each time you interact with the same person, relate to her or him as if it's the first time. Don't get stuck in fixed ideas or old habits. Similarly, each time you tackle a task you've done before, approach it as if it were the first time.

Interact with people each time as if it's the first time.

Although you feel you've done the same assignment dozens of times before, rethink the situation each time from scratch, even briefly.

I tried to reinvent procedures when I worked for the international management consulting company I mentioned back in the introduction. Although I had heaps of past material to use as models in the communication projects I carried out, rather than follow the standard format and change a few details, I invented new approaches.

This made the work more interesting and, I felt, yielded better results.

Remaining receptive challenges our spirit and our zest for life. Consider, for example, the plight of a city councilor attending public meetings day after day, receiving numerous delegations and submissions. Public officials hear the same arguments, often from the same people, over and over again. It's tempting to shut these people off or at least to close one's ears and mind. Why bother paying attention to tedious, repeated complaints? But as the cynicism grows, fresh thinking evaporates. Valid insights and innovative solutions, even if seldom revealed in such irksome circumstances, are missed. Opportunities to break through are foregone. Somehow, people charged with public office must fight this tendency and learn to remain open-minded and responsive.

We all need to practice allowing our minds to continually reinvent and renew, training ourselves to break old habits. (For myself, it's a lifelong task.) No matter how often you've done the same kind of project before, addressed a similar topic, or reasoned with the same person – your child, for instance, or a coworker – learn to treat each situation as new and fresh. Ongoing reinvention opens your eyes to details and dimensions previously missed and to conditions that are forever changing. Assuming things remain the same blocks your vision and insight. Communication and creativity require freshness, even when new ideas are grounded in tradition.

Break habits and reinvent continually.

Although you feel you've done the same assignment dozens of times before, rethink the situation each time from scratch, even briefly. Don't assume anything. Ask yourself basic questions like, What's the key purpose? Who's this for? What are the objectives? Take nothing for granted. Don't necessarily do a project the same way

you've done it before. Doing so again and again saps your
energy and confidence.

Rethink
repeated tasks
from scratch.

Instead, reexamine and reinvent. Ongoing reinvention
stimulates your natural creative powers and sustains personal satisfaction. In turn, your creativity arouses other
people's interest. Approaching everything freshly, you
find within yourself the strength and insight to see new
possibilities and create new solutions.

Reality inspires creativity

In my own life, as tempted as I often am to rely on
"old wheels" to carry me through difficult circumstances, I don't think it works. Difficulties are inevitable.
Throughout our lives we regularly find ourselves facing
adversity, often alone and particularly at times of loss or
crisis when we lack our customary resources or can't rely
on old ways of doing things. If you've realized, however,
that you can reinvent the wheel at each juncture of your
life, you can meet these crises head on with the confidence to adjust to if not overcome your problems.

Find strength
in facing situa-
tions freshly.

Reinventing the wheel is a powerful way to build
self-confidence and find a deeper source of strength and
stability. Ordinarily, stability is seen as holding on to the
old ways of doing things and maintaining the status quo.
But this is a response from fear: the fear that if we don't
hold onto what we have now, we'll become powerless
and impoverished tomorrow. If, instead, you find confidence in your inherent ability to constantly recreate and
reinvent, then your stability arises not from holding on
but from trusting yourself.

So the next time someone laughs at you for rethinking
an old problem or taking a new approach to communicating something that's already been formulated and done
before, just smile to yourself and keep on wheeling.

One important caveat: reinventing the wheel does not mean being original for originality's sake alone. We can make big mistakes when we change things merely for the sake of change, when we reinvent wheels merely because we're tired of the old ones. Doing new things is fine, but don't confuse novelty with your true power of creativity. You reinvent the wheel not to get anywhere, but to get somewhere.

Reinventing the wheel is a powerful way to build self-confidence and find a deeper source of strength and stability.

Deal genuinely with each situation as it arises. When you have a problem, respond to it with fresh insight to the circumstances you face, who you are, and the resources you possess. Creativity arises not from an imaginary universe outside of reality, but from your active response to real-life situations. Understanding this distinction is critical, for in it lies the very essence of communication and creativity: to perceive and respond appropriately to the moment. Even the most wildly creative art emerges from the artist's intersection with the real world.

Truly speaking, we are all artists – makers of things and ideas. When you approach a new but repeated task, like writing a report, take as your objective not just doing it differently from before. Look into the topic honestly, see it with a fresh mind, and create what suits the circumstances. Creativity arises not from some fiction but from

reality – a reality you're totally part of. Reinventing the
wheel is the natural act of being alive.

YOUR STORY

When was the last time someone said to you, or
you said, "Don't reinvent the wheel," or similar
words? Rethink the situation. Did you go ahead
anyway and come up with a new approach and
try something different? Or were you derailed
from seeing the situation in a fresh light and devising a better, more creative solution? Write up
your experience in a short paragraph and send it
to www.WordsBecomeYou.com. Tell coworkers
about the site and see how they react to your story.

6

Order Chaos

Writing well gives you an edge in whatever work you do. Here are some specific tips on how to organize all the information you've collected and express it clearly – how to find order in chaos.

AT THIS POINT IN THE BOOK you might be thinking, Thanks for all the philosophy. But how can I actually organize material and produce something that communicates clearly? Give me some practical tips on how to create orderly, meaningful communication from what seems like a random mess of information and ideas.

The short answer is – have faith: faith that things do make sense, and that you have the ability to see and express information coherently. This chapter sets out a number of specific techniques for applying this conviction and creating form.

As mentioned in the introduction, communication skills give you an edge in whatever work you do. Here I focus on writing because fewer people nowadays seem able to write fluently. Improving your composition skills broadens your horizons. Even if you don't need to improve your writing, the techniques presented here will help you build your facility for organizing any complex material or task.

Everyone faces complexity. Businesspeople. Scientists. Theologians. Politicians. Plumbers. Parents. Teenagers. Even experienced professional writers — it certainly applies to me — feel overwhelmed having to organize and compose their work. Complexity is inevitable because everything in life *is* complex, or at least seems so. Look at any issue closely enough and you'll encounter contradictions and permutations. Yet within this chaos a natural order exists. But how to find it?

The key, as I said, is to learn to trust that you already possess an innate faculty for uncovering the order that exists in chaos, whether in the natural world or the world of ideas. Your mind instinctively perceives order. Your visual perception, for example, distinguishes between individual shapes, though in reality there's a mass of visual detail in front of you. Similarly, at the conscious level your mind naturally thinks and conceives in discrete blocks even though millions of brain cells are firing away. Why? Because you have the power of clarity.

When you first encounter a forest, you see an apparently random mass of trees and you think "trees." Up closer you spot a single tree. Approaching it, first you see only a random mass of leaves. From closer yet you realize that each branch has a recurring pattern of leaves, with minor variations. You begin to perceive the rhythmic relationships and natural harmonies from forest to tree to leaf. Seeing the patterns makes it easier to share your perceptions about the forest and its components.

The old saying "Can't see the forest for the trees" speaks of getting so lost in details that you can't see the whole picture. The opposite predicament also limits vision. When you "Can't see the trees for the forest," you feel so overwhelmed with the whole that you can't relate to the details.

Life is rich in both details and wholeness, individualities and patterns. They're not contradictory. Singularity and multiplicity coexist in an ever-changing dynamic of life's unfolding story. And like any story, it has a narrative, a storyline. Within any mass of ideas and materials from which you must create coherency, your mind can find relationships – a story. The trees and leaves are forever stirring in the wind, evolving and changing in their environment. Yet a beautiful logic exists. All you need do is have faith in your ability to draw it out.

Look at any issue closely enough and you'll encounter contradictions and permutations. Yet within this chaos a natural order exists.

Don't be misled into thinking that this faith is magical or otherworldly. Science and mathematics as well as philosophy and religion all find systems of order in the face of what appears to be chaotic conglomerations of facts, phenomena, and ideas. You, too, can find order in your everyday life of thoughts and communication no matter how daunting the task.

Finding natural sequence

One of the tougher assignments I received was to write a biography about a prominent and powerful businessman, philanthropist, and sportsman. He pursued these and other endeavors not in discrete blocks of his life, dedicated to only one pursuit at a time, but simultaneously and continuously throughout his long life. How, I worried, could I organize the book into chapters that would make sense while also following a more-or-less chronological sequence?

Through an iterative process of digesting and outlining all the material I accumulated, a structure began to emerge that met both needs. I found, for example, that while my subject was deeply involved in thoroughbred horse racing all of his adult life, it made sense to have an earlier chapter about when he first owned and raced horses and a later chapter relating how he ended up controlling the entire racing industry in his region.

Similarly, his lifelong career in the meat business divided into distinct periods: when he first began to work on the shop floor of a slaughter house, later when he bought up a number of small butcher shops, and finally when he rose to become the largest meat processor around.

Instead of combining these stages into one section or, alternatively, writing the whole book in a strictly chronological order regardless of subject, I articulated each stage of his meat business but mixed the chapters sequentially with the other aspects of his life. This way the story came together both as a whole and in its parts.

This being the first book I ever wrote, let alone
my first biography, I felt overwhelmed by the scale
of work. But fortunately I'd gained enough confidence as a professional writer to know that order
would eventually emerge from the heap of material
I had assembled.

Integrating relationships

In an earlier chapter I explained how to synthesize a singular all-encompassing theme for a written document or
other form of communication. You can also use the power
synthesis to create organizational clarity. In synthesizing information you find a coherent new whole, an idea,
or a system by mixing and combining individual facts
and thoughts. Think of it as a kind of mental alchemy,
creating something new out of different elements.

Once you've determined the unifying theme for a
composition or other form of communication – or the
organizing principle for any task – a natural order may
also become evident, since the order should express and
elaborate on the central idea. More often, you'll need to
continue the process of synthesis in order to develop a
more complete structure for your work.

But remember, after conducting your research and
other inquiries and assembling your material, before
trying to organize it, pause and do something different.
Take a break. During this time, make note of any insights
or ideas for organizing your work that come to mind.
Record these thoughts no matter how inconsequential
or ridiculous they may seem at the moment or on subsequent reflection.

Later, if you feel the need, inquire further into your
subject and assemble more information. Take additional
breaks and keep making notes of your insights. As time

passes you'll find yourself with piles of notes recording random thoughts and perhaps the beginning of a rough outline.

Now enter into a staged, recurring process of reviewing and boiling all of your information down into an organized outline of your ideas and material. This is an iterative process: that is, you go through it again and again in a series or a repeated cycle, each time peeling away or adding new layers and finding new relationships, associations, and combinations, gradually building up a more and more orderly structure. Things fall into focus. Clarity emerges.

> *The web of life is a never-ending drama (tragedy/comedy, your pick) of interrelated causes and effects.*

Don't worry about finding the "truth" or making it perfect. And you don't have to worry about showing your work to anyone at this point. Simply look for ways to combine the various elements of your subject into a coherent grouping or flow of ideas. See how some elements fit together with others in different and related levels of topics. Play with your material. Try different hierarchies and structures for organizing the topics. Move items back and forth until things fall into place and a logic emerges that feels right.

Build structure using associations and hierarchies.

Remember you can always remix and redo your organizational structure as it develops. It's not written in stone. Your structure is malleable and adaptable. It's your tool. The iterative process should feel cozy not intimidating.

Rather than worrying about being correct, simply consider how ideas can be lumped together; or, more accurately, discover how they naturally fall together. And later, when you do the actual writing, don't feel bound to stick precisely to the structure you developed. While writing you'll often find that steps are missing and must be added in, or you'll suddenly see clearer ways to arrange and sequence the information. No problem, your outline only serves as a guide.

Rest assured, above all, that somewhere within the collection of stuff you've accumulated, everything is, in fact, related. This web of relationship is not supernatural: things *are* related. The web of life is a never-ending drama (tragedy/comedy, your pick) of interrelated causes and effects.

Feel free to change your outline later, while you write.

We see this writ large in the universe looking through powerful telescopes at the explosions within great nebulae, and we see it in the ecology of our planet. The web of life is so complex and interrelated, and we're all so utterly a part of it, we can never see its nature completely. We only get glimpses.

Enough about philosophy. You don't need to fret about perfection or the universe or the world of neutrinos and electrons to find order in chaos. Your job is to communicate clearly. As you go through the process of reviewing your material, simply trust that a logic or order will begin to emerge and take shape.

Here's a very important caveat. Don't get misled into thinking or fearing that only one natural order exists and that you must find it. This is a dictatorship of the mind and spirit. And it's false. Any set of information or ideas can be organized in different ways. There's no single correct order. Order itself keeps changing. As I've already suggested, don't get hung up looking for the one truth. That's not the point. The point is that your brain, your very being, has an inherent capacity for finding order, making sense, and then communicating.

You need your skeleton

The word *outline* has appeared several times in this chapter. It astonishes me how often people attempt to write something without first outlining their ideas. You can, of course, write powerful communications without organizing in advance what you want to say. When you want to express your feelings in a love letter, for instance, let your thoughts and emotions pour out rather than deliberately planning what you're going to say.

However, even a love letter should be checked and perhaps edited before you send if off. We often say the craziest things in times of passion or strong emotion that are meaningful to us in the moment but leave a mistaken impression. Many relationships, not just romantic ones, have broken up over disastrously abrupt and unchecked letters. It's happened to me more than once. E-mail notes in particular are problematic because we've been lulled by their instantaneous transmittal into composing and sending them without any second thought or review.

An experienced writer may be able to write without a detailed plan of action, having developed a practiced skill for the art and process of organization. But even professional writers usually make some kind of plan before they put pen to paper or fingers to keys. A plan or outline shows whether a chosen approach to organizing a topic makes sense or not, and then serves as the skeleton to which you attach the meat of the matter.

Even if I haven't already made an outline but find that my writing isn't flowing, I step back and compose one. I might start by reviewing what I've written so far, making a list showing a key word or phrase for each sequential

Use outlines to organize your work.

paragraph. Doing this usually reveals a break in the logical flow and a better way to proceed.

Long ago I gave a course on report writing to a firm of urban planning consultants. Before the first lesson, I looked over some of their recent reports and noted their disorderliness. Later, when I was standing at the blackboard, explaining how to develop an outline, it suddenly hit me that these of all people ought to understand the importance of planning ahead. I turned to them and said, "Hey, planners – plan! Think ahead with your written communication just as you do when formulating a sensible, thought-out planned approach to urban development."

The blank page or blank screen is far less intimidating and far easier to fill when you work from a plan.

Nearly all of us need a plan, whether we're going out shopping, tackling a difficult project, or writing something. You'll find that the blank page or blank screen is far less intimidating and far easier to fill when you work from a plan rather than relying solely on your memory or inspiration. You can still allow your thoughts to pour out while you're writing. But at least you have an outline to propel you, or to fall back on.

Following a plan makes work less intimidating.

After writing, you can review your outline (or outlines, for often you may have produced more than one list) to crosscheck that you've covered everything you intended to. This is a trick I've employed successfully for years. I don't worry while I'm writing if I'm covering everything I intended to because I know I'll check back on my outline and other notes after I've finished the first draft.

While I'm actually writing I let the words flow, often ignoring my outline altogether. If you've worked long enough on your material, researching and synthesizing it, you can trust that the plan is already imbedded in your mind. Moreover, in the process of writing, new ideas and new sequences naturally arise. Don't block this flow because it appears to violate the outline you developed earlier. Your power of clarity is not fixed but flexible.

In other words, don't be precious about your structure. Use it but don't hesitate to change it in the course of producing your document or other communication. An outline provides you with a tool, not a bible. Similarly with any kind of task: strategies change when you're engaged in doing the actual work.

Review your lists to check if everything's been covered.

Nevertheless, don't forget to make a plan, even if it's just a shortlist of thoughts. Outlines can take the form of elaborate, hierarchical structures using formal methods of numbering, or look more like a shopping list with short bulleted items. Do what works for you.

A to K: Eleven tips for getting clear

Once you have a sense of order, you then face the challenge of expressing yourself with clarity in whatever medium you're working in. For a detailed review of grammar, syntax, style, and format, you can consult any number of excellent textbooks. Or, better yet, buy a copy of that marvelous, short book Strunk & White's *Elements of Style*. I've never found a reference that so succinctly explains the essentials of written composition. I read it over again every few years to remind myself of its basic yet often forgotten principles.

In the remainder of this chapter I highlight a number of techniques that have long worked especially well for me. These organizational and composition practices may not coincide entirely with the rules you were taught in school. Most of us were given ironclad directives like, Don't split infinitives! These are myths to be shed. (By the way, for a fascinating mini-essay on the subject of split infinitives, consult the entry in *Fowler's Modern English Usage,* another classic reference book.)

The best way to develop your eye and ear for correct and expressive language usage is to read a great deal of good writing.

Grammatical and composition rules should not be followed blindly. Most are sensible and important. You must, however, also cultivate your own ability to discriminate and write appropriately to match the situation and express what you wish to communicate. Sometimes, to cite just one example, infinitives can be broken to express adequately your meaning. Wait a moment. That didn't sound right! To adequately express your meaning... Now that sounds more straightforward and natural.

Don't follow grammar rules blindly.

The best way to develop your eye and ear for correct and expressive language usage is to read a great deal of good writing, including books and magazines. Reading voluminously throughout life cultivates the linguistic synapses of your brain and builds fluency. Remember, though. that writing evolved from spoken language, not the other way around. Written material, even when more formal, makes the most sense when it evokes as much meaning and intention when you read it aloud in an inflected voice.

Here, then, is my personal list of techniques for achieving clarity.

A – Emphasize key points

When you want to emphasize something, use the beginning or the ending whether in a sentence, paragraph, or whole composition. This applies to all media, written, spoken, and visual.

People typically pay more attention to the beginnings and endings of things, often skipping the middle or forgetting it by the time they've finished. Mind you, I didn't say, "State your whole point at the beginning" or "Lay out all your cards right at the start." How much you reveal depends on the circumstances. But you can use the start and finish to focus on an issue or call attention to it.

Some authorities will tell you that the beginning receives the most attention and the ending the second most. This isn't always true. It varies according to the circumstance. Sometimes the ending leaves a sharper memory. But other times people may not make it to the end of what you've written, and you can only rely on leaving a first impression. The beginning or opening is so important in writing that the next chapter is dedicated entirely to its effective use.

Use beginnings and endings to make your main points.

B – Layer levels of detail

People generally cannot assimilate a mass of detail from written material or other communication, and certainly not without being given a coherent context. One way to create context is to layer your information into levels of detail. Beginning with a more general level helps people picture things clearly from the start; they can see a path ahead and then go as deeply as they want through the subsequent layers. The layering provides your audience with a context as they delve into the details.

You can do this within each paragraph or section and also more basically in how you structure a whole document or other form of communication, be it an article, report, exhibit, slide show, or lecture. Begin by stating a general principle or main idea, then follow with deeper and deeper layers of information or explanation. How many layers or how deep to go – and how to structure the specific levels or hierarchies – depends on the particular subject, medium, and audience. You may also need to re-state your general idea here and there to keep the context evident throughout your document or presentation.

Layering can take any number of forms. Don't be misled by another one of those high school myths: that all paragraphs must begin with one thought which you then expand on in three or five sentences, followed by a conclusion. The actual form of layering within a paragraph or within a whole document should fit the circumstances.

Other layering devices you can use to create context in a written document include introductions, summaries at the start of each chapter, sidebars, and an index. In this book, in addition to the above, I've placed short notes along the side of the main text to summarize key points. Magazines and exhibits do something similar by enticing readers with compelling extracts or pull-quotes taken from an article's main text, another device I've employed here.

C – Communicate with headings

The principle of layering also applies to headings. People often miss an opportunity to communicate by leaving out headings altogether or by using them only to announce

Create context by layering information.

the subject of each section. Effective headings and sub-headings function in two ways: they convey a sense of organization, logic, and context – in other words, clarity – to your material; and they may be all that a reader sees. Write with both purposes in mind.

Organize and compose your headings to help your readers see the logic and flow of your thinking. This also makes it easier for them to find what they may be looking for. In case your audience doesn't bother to read anything further, write your headings so that on their own they convey your main messages.

Write headings that tell a story.

Ideally, headings should actually say something in partial or complete phrases. They can always be supplemented if necessary with simpler, subject-type headings at a secondary level. But if you only use a basic subject – like *clarity* or *synthesis* – as a heading, you haven't exploited the opportunity to get your main point across. To repeat, readers rely on headings for a sense of order and for choosing what to read. The headings may also be the only thing they see.

Here's another tip: Write the headings so that they work regardless of whether someone reads them sequentially from start to finish, skips around randomly, or reads from the back to the front. (Think of how often you flip through a magazine starting at the back.) Like it or not, this is how people often read, and even more so nowadays when they read – or *surf*, as it's aptly called – through websites, riding the waves rapidly from one site to another.

But consider also a far older medium, the newspaper, and its traditional use of headings, subheadings, and what are called *decks*, the highlighted introductory paragraphs. All three of these levels are written to seduce readers into delving deeper. They also help people choose what they want to read and give them some information or an impression in case they don't read everything in detail.

Trade shows and exhibitions work the same way, with attendees typically wandering around from one display to another. Very few people go through exhibits systematically, reading everything in a linear fashion. Instead, they notice powerful images and large main headings. If these catch their attention, they may read a secondary level of text. And if they're really captivated, they might linger a little longer and read a third level of more detailed explanation.

Your writing or any other form of communication ideally should be designed and the text written so that the audience gets something regardless of how deeply they steep themselves in your material and regardless of what order they look at it.

D – Make relationships explicit

You communicate more clearly, particularly in formal reports, when a document's structure itself explicitly highlights important relationships, such as between objectives and findings or between key issues and solutions. You can do this with your headings, for example, by using the same or similar wording both in your objectives and in subsequent chapters and conclusions pertaining to those objectives. Readers are alerted to the relationships when the headings echo earlier wording.

Design your structure to make relationships apparent.

Writers often fail to draw out such relationships clearly, as if embarrassed to make things too obvious or fearful of oversimplifying their arguments. But clear and effective communication requires simplification. Certainly remain true to your material; don't falsify, mislead, or cover up complexity. At the same time, helping readers see the relationships helps them sift through masses of information.

E – Keep parallel and consistent

In headings, lists, and other format devices, try to use parallel wording and syntax. Notice, for example, how this book's chapter headings and nearly all the side notes consistently use the imperative voice.

If you vary a form, you risk dislodging your readers' comprehension and losing their attention. Even a momentary loss of attention can derail a reader's interest. Don't be pious in applying this (or any) rule, however; be judicious. Sometimes variation is needed for emphasis or clarity, or just to provide relief from tedium. As a general rule, however, parallel structure aids comprehension.

Use parallel wording and format to aid comprehension.

Parallelism and clarity are also achieved by using consistent style and language. If you decide to start chapters with short summaries, for example, don't suddenly have a chapter without one. It would jar your readers and leave them doubting your reliability.

Also be consistent in your use of tense, person, and general tone. But, again, don't feel driven to make your writing absolutely uniform; instead, strive to be consistently inconsistent. So, for example, in this book, fairly regularly although not consistently, I alternate between using the pronoun *we* when I'm talking about people's habits in general and *you* when I'm offering specific advice. Another caveat: don't carry this rule so far that your writing becomes dry. Variation if used judiciously and consciously, not capriciously, can keep your readers awake and interested.

F – Avoid fanciness and jargon

Somewhere along the way, many people are left with the impression that complicated or indirect wording makes them appear smarter or impresses their readers with a subject's importance. Not so. Straightforward language conveys ideas more clearly and memorably. Sentences that get

bogged down in indirect language should be rethought
and rewritten. It's difficult to catch every awkward sentence in your writing – I'm sure I've missed some in this
book despite how many times as I've checked for them.
Just do the best you can.

Another reason some people employ complicated and
indirect wording is to cushion or cover up something
they don't want to say openly or to hide the fact that
they don't know what they're talking about. In the latter
case, more research is required, or the subject should be
dropped. In the former case, write diplomatically not by
covering something up but by showing respect for the
audience; in other words, use sincere finesse. Be honest
with yourself as well as your readers: say what you want
to say plainly, or don't say it at all.

When you find yourself stuck trying again and again
to write something clearly, try a simple technique I've
used successfully for years. Ask yourself – possibly aloud
– What exactly am I trying to say here? Then answer the
question, immediately and aloud, and without thinking
about it. Write down exactly what first comes to mind.
You'll be surprised how often this will break an impasse
and lead you to express your subject more cogently and
with simple and straightforward language.

Taking that further, learn to think of writing as being
more like speaking. (This point is important enough to
warrant a chapter of its own, which follows later.) Most
people tend to speak more simply and straightforwardly
than they write. Writing is, of course, a more formal
mode of communication than speaking. Nevertheless,
don't let formality turn into stiffness.

In a similar vein, there's no excuse for using jargon.
Our language is rich with ordinary words you can use
instead of specialized or arcane words known only to
a small group of peers. Academics and other specialists

Use straight-forward language.

Ask yourself, What exactly am I trying to say here.

Think of writing as more like speaking.

sometimes think they must use technical terms to express highly specific concepts or facts. Sometimes they must; many disciplines do have specialized vocabularies. But in my experience relying on jargon often comes from habit or serves as an excuse for not making the extra effort to think of a more direct and comprehensible way to say something. In fact, figuring out direct and more ordinary language often helps bring clarity to a subject – and not only for your readers but also for yourself. The best technical and scientific writing avoids jargon no matter how narrow the audience.

Generally speaking, also aim where possible and accurate to use shorter words, typically of Anglo-Saxon origin, rather than longer fancy-seeming alternatives, typically of Latin origin. Shorter words convey ideas directly and with greater spirit. Why, for example, would you say *Avail yourself of diminutive vocabulary,* when you could simply say *Use shorter words*? Fancy words do not impress; they jar the reader and make you seem pretentious.

G – Feel the rhythm

Having too many short or long sentences in a row puts readers to sleep. Thoughtfully mixing the length and syntax of sentences keeps readers awake. It also gives you another technique: generally speaking, use longer sentences to draw out deeper more complex relationships; use shorter sentences to summarize or emphasize key points. Sentences have rhythm in how they are phrased and also in their length. Varying the length adds character and sharpness to your writing.

Mix short and long sentences.

H – Speak with a strong voice

Sometimes you need to use passive voice to make a point clear or, for emphasis, to put the subject at the end of a sentence. Active voice, however, usually communicates more sharply and directly. In other words, your meaning is more clearly communicated by you if it is actively voiced. Right. But how about saying more simply, You communicate your meaning more clearly by using active voice. When you realize that your writing has become indirect and awkward, think of how to say the same thing with fewer words. This will usually lead you to employ active voice, transitive verbs, and stronger vocabulary.

Intransitive verbs – *to be, is, are,* and so on – are not as forceful as active voice and transitive verbs. Better yet, I should say, Active, transitive verbs convey meaning more forcefully than do intransitive verbs.

Favor active voice and transitive verbs.

Sometimes you have to use intransitive verbs to draw out your meaning. But repeated use of "to be" verbs puts readers to sleep. Try to notice when you're relying on these weaker verbs or the passive voice repeatedly and look for more active ways to say the same things. Here, too, develop a feeling for rhythm in your writing.

I – Consult good sources

Get into the habit of using good references – dictionaries, a thesaurus, phrase books, style manuals, and so on. A few classics have already been mentioned, including Strunk & White's *Elements of Style* and *Fowler's Modern English Usage.* Another book I regularly use is *The Chicago Manual of Style.* It answers just about every possible format and style question you can think of.

Also consult specialized reference books. From time to time, for example, I use a small book that lists correct word divisions and another that shows the appropriate prepositions to use with verbs. Find the reference books that meet your particular needs.

Consult reference books for specific needs.

With computer technology and the Internet, we have whole new reference resources available to us with only a few clicks of a key or mouse. Many are built into word processing and e-mail programs. Take care, however, not to rely exclusively on these seductive digital tools. Classic reference books often provide more numerous and precise alternatives. For example, I still use my old ragged copy of *Roget's International Thesaurus* to find synonyms; it provides more choices and more precision than what's offered within a word-processing program.

J – Get unstuck using "tricks"

When you find yourself with a seriously flawed or unsatisfactory first draft and you can't see your way to fix it, here's a technique ("a trick of the trade") that helps me get unstuck. Go through your draft paragraph by paragraph and on a separate piece of paper list the subject of each paragraph using a couple of words or a short phrase – sort of like outlining after the fact. Reviewing this will help you to see where you're stuck and what could work as a better organization.

As well, you'll often find it far more efficient to rewrite something from scratch than to scratch your head for hours trying to fix something that's bogged down. Your next draft will flow more freely. Try it.

Don't slave over weak drafts; rewrite them.

You can also get unstuck with troublesome drafts and avoid being intimidated by large projects if you break them up into a series of smaller sections, much like you would tear up a slice of bread instead of shoving the whole thing into your mouth. Completing a project section by section gives you a sense of growing satisfaction. Moreover, you can skip problematic parts and return to them when, in the context of having the others done, things become clearer and the job, less daunting. Remember the old dictum "Divide and conquer."

Break projects into digestible chunks.

With the biography I mentioned earlier in this chapter, by focusing on and ticking off chapters one by one as I finished them in turn, the large, formidable project didn't feel so intimidating. I also followed my own advice, skipping a couple of troublesome chapters until the rest of the work was completed.

Yet another trick you can try if you're stuck figuring out what to write or how to say something is to pretend that whatever it is – for example, a title, a visual image, or a whole outline – has already been created and produced. Close your eyes and picture the finished item in front of you. What's the first thing you see? Don't dismiss anything that arises. Use your imagination freely. You can employ this technique in any aspect of your life, whether you're thinking of a dish to cook for dinner or imaging where you want to take your next vacation. Close your eyes and see what appears.

Close your eyes and visualize the solution.

K – Rely on other eyes

The value of having your final draft reviewed by someone else, particularly a good editor, cannot be overstated. People are often surprised that, even though I'm a professional writer, I employ freelance copyeditors to review my own writing.

When you work for a long time preparing a document or any other form of communication, you develop blind spots, so to speak. Each time you read through your draft, you're partly reading through memory; you're not freshly seeing what you've written. As a result, you may not spot awkward wording or outright spelling and grammatical mistakes. Spellcheckers and grammar checkers do not spot every error, and their corrections are not consistently correct.

Ask others to review your final draft.

Don't be upset by a reviewer's suggestions. Remain objective instead of letting your ego get in the way. You can always accept, reject, or modify a suggestion or criticism. Don't take it personally but as an opportunity to see things with someone else's eyes. Besides, many pairs of eyes will be looking at your work once you release it; so you might as well get some reaction ahead of time.

After rewriting or revising, before sending your work out (especially when preparing a particularly important document), get into the habit of calling again on a second or third pair of eyes to review it. Also be sure that each time a proof comes back from a printer or designer to check it yet again. Mistakes creep into proofs — for that matter, mistakes creep into all aspects of life — for a myriad of reasons. So check and recheck.

But don't become a nervous wreck worrying about finding every error; they happen; we learn from them. Just stay relaxed and focused, and rely on your natural power of clarity, finding order in chaos.

YOUR STORY

Do you have any special tricks or techniques you use to organize tasks, written or otherwise? Do you outline your projects ahead of time? Describe briefly how you make sense out of complicated material or how you might do it next time. Send your ideas to www.WordsBecomeYou.com.

7

Start with the End

Don't wait until the end of a work to articulate your main idea or conclusion. Give people a frame of reference at the beginning so they have a context for the rest of what you say. But handle it with finesse.

WHATEVER KIND OF COMMUNICATION or project you're delivering, begin by articulating your main point or goal right at the start.

Whoa! Wait a second. That's a pretty bold thing to say. How can you state your main point before you build the case for it? Why would anyone bother reading or listening any further once you've given everything away? Worse yet, if you're trying to promote something controversial and have to convince others of its merit, why risk alienating them at the beginning? They'll close their minds to everything you say afterwards.

These are sound points. You don't want to give everything away and risk losing your audience's attention. You also don't want to alienate them to the point that they ignore you. You must build a strong case to get your message across convincingly.

Nevertheless, people need a "hook" right at the start not just to pull them in but so that they have something literally to hang on to, something to give them bearing. People require a perspective, a window, from which to perceive and appreciate – and even be convinced by – all of what you have to say. How you state your main point at the start, however, must be done deftly, with skill and sensitivity to the particular message and audience. This is the power of articulation.

Like most people, I often hesitate to say exactly what I feel or think at the start of a conversation. I'm more comfortable leaving it till the end, fearful that I might upset people or not convince them if I don't build my argument first. But I've learned to overcome this shyness because I've seen over and over again that people are not alienated if I'm frank with them – and particularly so if I'm sensitive to where they're coming from.

Even if they disagree with my position, openness and honesty from the start sets the stage for genuine dialogue. Besides, I know that if I leave my main point till the end I may never get there, for people may have lost interest by then or time may have run out. Better to "start with the end," to articulate right at the beginning what I'm tempted to leave until later.

MY STORY

Moving finish to front

"Starting with the end" can work quite literally. During the years I ran an international journal on automobile accidents and injuries, often the first thing I did when I edited a contributor's article was to move what had been the concluding paragraph to the beginning. The wording often required some adjustment to read coherently as an introduction rather than a conclusion. But this one simple modi-fication, starting the essay off with the conclusion rather than leaving it to the end, frequently brought the entire article into clearer focus.

All of our articles were moderately technical but the audience came from many professions, so the pieces had to be edited to work for everyone. Providing a context at the start of each article helped readers to understand the full contents, particularly when a subject was outside their own field. Without that context, many readers might have missed the significance of an article and skipped over it. Even if they chose not to read further, at least they got the gist right away.

Here are some examples of opening paragraphs drawn from the magazine:

Drivers' risk of crashing increases fourfold while they are using a mobile phone. This fairly dramatic finding is the single most important conclusion of a study I recently completed. The increase in risk is remarkably consistent, remaining the same in the summer and winter, daytime and nighttime, and for each day of the week.

[Although the opening here gives away the study's principal finding before it's elaborated, the striking conclusion itself arouses interest.]

In every trial the facts have to be found and they are often an elusive quarry hidden in circuitous paths behind brambles of contradictory evidence. Self-interest tends to modify stark truth. As H.L. Mencken observed: "It is hard to believe that a man is telling the truth when you know that you would lie if you were in his place."

[This metaphorical opening is bolstered by the blunt words of a legendary social observer from the past.]

Do babies and children feel pain differently from adults? Research evidence shows that pain poses a greater risk of noxious effects and long-term damage for newborn and premature babies.

> [The initial paragraph here raises the article's basic question and also gives the answer, but without giving it all away.]

Swarms of motorcycles hovering around my car, storming into the Taipei intersection the instant the signal turns green...Tens of thousands of people in one Tokyo district after another...Thirty-five minutes to travel a single Bangkok block...Whirling in a taxi through interlaced roads across a densely populated Central Hong Kong hillside...Paying to enter Singapore's manicured downtown.

> [Although the article's theme isn't mentioned, the first paragraph entices readers with brief, colorful descriptions of the various locales covered in the ensuing piece.]

Forty years ago, when the U.S. Emergency Medical Services system was first developed, it was intended primarily to treat adult trauma and cardiac patients. No special protocols existed for handling seriously ill and injured children. But children aren't just small adults, and when they're injured they must have emergency care specifically tailored to their needs.

> [The opening in this example sets the thesis in an historical context.]

The secret to avoiding crashes is a combination of attention, motivation, and training...right?

> [To set up an argument contrary to conventional thinking, stating something typically taken for granted is followed by the slightly teasing question "right?".]

Building bridges

We generally avoid articulating our conclusion or main point until the end of whatever it is we're doing for one of four reasons: We hesitate revealing our position until we've first made a case for it. We refrain from saying anything too decisive for fear of alienating people. We don't, in fact, know what to conclude. Or, most commonly, especially with technical or specialized communication, we don't realize that what we write or say isn't clear to everyone.

Let's look at the last scenario first. Most of us get so caught up in our own situation and thoughts that we assume, without perhaps knowing we're assuming it, that whatever it is we have to say everyone else will find interesting and understandable, or that others will naturally think the same way we do.

If you want to reach out to people, you must create an intersection between your cosmos and theirs.

We each tend to live in our own little cosmos of reality and think that whatever we think is important *is* most important. It's not necessarily that we're selfish or ignorant. Maybe we're just so enthusiastic we forget that others are also running around feeling encased in their own little cosmos. We, the author or speaker or leader, implicitly understand the logic and value of what we're talking about; we're intimate with the topic. But we forget that others aren't.

If you want to reach out to people, you must create an intersection between your cosmos and theirs. Somehow you must open up a channel or build a bridge that connects otherwise seemingly separate universes of perception and value. That's not to say that people don't perceive things similarly. They do. In the great scheme of things, people see things quite similarly, especially if they're from the same culture. Even people from differing cultures share more in common and see things more similarly than they might at first think.

But people are busy; they have their own agendas and **Establish** priorities. Their minds are occupied with other things **a context** than your concerns. They need to relate cogently to your **your audience** context if you hope to reach out to them, draw them into **relates to.** dialogue, and enlist their support and cooperation. When cultures differ between people, establishing a context becomes even more critical.

So think of your opening words or remarks as a bridge. You need to create a connection for people to approach what you have to say and enter into understanding. Stating your main point at the start is one of the strongest ways to do this.

That doesn't mean that you have to give everything away or state your conclusions nakedly. Sometimes yes, sometimes no. It depends on the circumstances. But think it through from other people's perspective. What would attract their interest, and what would help them at the start to make sense out of the rest of your document, speech, audio-visual, or other form of presentation?

Say what you're going to say

A friend of mine who was a top executive in the advertising world likes to tell the story of his rector who would start out his sermons saying, "I'm going to tell you three things. I'm going to tell you them three times. And I'm going to be out of here in ten minutes."

Here's a perfect example that giving away the main point at the start may not consist, literally, of giving anything away. But the effect is the same. The rector set up his audience to pay attention by saying rather humorously that he was going to deliver his talk in a particular sequence and do it quickly. In a certain respect, a determination to communicate clearly and quickly *was* his main point.

The rector's words were a variant of a well-known maxim on how to give presentations effectively: Say what you're going to say, say it, and then say what you've said. This sets out a highly structural approach to presenting your thoughts so that your audience can absorb and later recall your main points. Generally, it's good advice. But don't take it too literally.

There are, in fact, countless ways to launch something. For example, besides relying on your opening sentences and paragraphs to provide a set-up, you can use abstracts or other forms of introduction or even subtitles to position your main point or perspective and to support your opening sentences. Remember, though, that readers skip around and don't always read sequentially.

In the opening itself, whether written or spoken, you can ask a leading question that establishes the subject or problem and perhaps goes as far as pointing to the likely conclusion – the conclusion you want to make later. You can seduce your audience's interest by giving a hint of your conclusion, a bit of a tease. You can appear naive, mysterious, bold, deceptive, angry, or funny.

> Compose an opening that suits both audience and message.

In other words, determine according to the nature of your subject, audience, and medium what tone to use at the start and what exactly to say. Remember as well to consider carefully that your audience does not likely see things as you do even if you think they do. They need a perspective, a handle, a window from which to watch the rest of your act. The power of articulation encompasses both your own viewpoint and that of your audience.

Sharing points of view

But what if your conclusion is so controversial you risk alienating people by speaking boldly? How do you prepare others to receive your arguments or perspectives? The short answer is, manage such situations with finesse. For example, you can cushion your conclusion or main point by setting it into a broader context with which your readers, listeners, or observers can identify if not agree. By establishing a deeper level of commonality with people you can broach topics or present conclusions they might otherwise refuse to acknowledge or even hear at all.

Cushion controversy with commonality.

When you know what you want to say and state it clearly at the start, your writing flows far more easily.

Establishing a shared understanding of a topic in itself helps others to find a basis for communication, resolving disagreements, and setting out on shared courses of action. This is a technique used in successful dialogue as opposed to debate: helping people to hear each other by creating a degree of common understanding, or at least mutual sympathy.

What if the reasoning behind your topic or document is itself the main thing that needs to be communicated?

If you put the conclusion first won't you derail the logical sequence? The mistaken idea here is that argument must precede conclusion. This thinking is reinforced by the scientific method, the belief system of modern times: conclusions must be based on solid evidence and therefore the evidence must come first.

But there's no inherent reason you can't first say what it is you found out and then explain your reasoning. Giving people the conclusion first helps them to follow along as you then present the whole story step by step. Otherwise, you risk leaving your readers or listeners wondering what it is you're talking about.

Feel free to start with your conclusion.

Which reminds me of another story my advertising friend tells. Two guys come out of church and one asks the other, "How did you like the sermon?" "It reminded me of the love of God," the fellow answered. "It surpassed all understanding, and I thought it would go on forever." Maybe this rector should have stopped while he was ahead by just giving his conclusion and no more.

Of course, maybe he didn't have a conclusion; maybe he didn't even know what to say – another of the reasons I cited earlier why people often avoid stating their main point at the start. "People," by the way, includes me.

Sometimes under the pressure of completing an assignment, I plough ahead with the writing. Only later do I admit to myself that I don't really know what I'm talking about. I'm merely floating along, adding words onto more words, paragraphs onto paragraphs, lacking any anchor. Perhaps eventually, my main point begins to emerge from the process of writing itself.

I have two choices then: either to do some reconstructive surgery, shifting around paragraphs or whole sections and grafting on a new introduction that sets up the piece clearly; or to start all over again, beginning with a sharper, clearer focus.

Reconsider
your opening
after finishing
your work.

I'm often tempted to follow the first course, anxious to finish the work and predisposed to preserve what I've already composed, or too lazy to trash it all and start from scratch. This is a mistake. Starting from scratch usually proves far more efficient than helter-skelter surgery. When you know what you want to say and state it clearly at the start, your writing flows far more easily. You can always go back and borrow sentences or whole sections that worked well in the earlier draft.

Developing the habit of starting off by articulating your main point or context forces you to face up to whether, in fact, you know what you want to say. Even if you later change your opening to reflect how your work actually takes shape, taking that first step gets you going with the right spirit.

If you find yourself totally unable to speak directly and boldly, if your power of articulation remains in hiding, the next chapter should help break the impasse.

YOUR STORY

Look at one or two recent documents you wrote. Read the first and last paragraphs. Try modifying one of your last paragraphs and shifting it to the start of that piece. Send an example of this, or an opening paragraph you're already satisfied with, to www.WordsBecomeYou.com.

8

Speak Your Truth

Personal conviction gives meaning and purpose to your communication – and to your whole life. True conviction, however, arises from direct relationship with the world around you. Find your connection.

PERSONAL CONVICTION DRIVES our desire and ability to relate meaningfully with our fellow beings. Speaking our truth gives power and purpose to communicating and living generally. By *personal conviction* I mean your direct relationship with the world around you and with a particular subject.

For myself, when I'm lacking personal connection or conviction, I find it difficult to start a project let alone complete it. My spirit has disappeared; my energy has evaporated. Whenever I face such a predicament, I take it as a signal to return to the heart of the matter.

Throughout my career, when I've felt confused about how to write something, when my outline and thinking seemed disorderly, or when I admitted to myself that my first draft was a total mess and that my ideas weren't flowing fluently, I learned to employ a simple technique. I put everything aside – and I mean *everything* – and ask myself this basic question: What am I really trying to say here?

In other words, What's the key point I want to make? What essentially am I trying to accomplish?

When you're stuck in your writing, ask yourself this same fundamental question. Then, without thinking too much about it, allow your deepest impulses and beliefs to rise to the surface.

Getting to the heart of the matter, however, requires more than identifying the fundamentals or believing in something blindly. Getting to the heart requires finding your own connection with whatever it is you're trying to express or achieve. What do you believe in and care about and why? What is your point of personal reference and relationship? How does this all manifest itself in meaning? Without conviction, we risk losing our way. Without conviction, what we say or do turns out confusing and mediocre.

When you're stuck in your writing, ask yourself, What am I really trying to say here?

But don't wait for writer's block or failing first drafts or hesitancy of any kind before finding meaning in what you're trying to achieve. Instead, develop an instinctive habit to find your personal connection when you first start each new endeavor. The more you work from a source of belief and identification, the stronger your communications and actions will be. Working from conviction gives clarity and energy to your life. It gives you greater satisfaction in both the process and the aftermath of work. If you genuinely care about something, you enjoy going

Find meaning at the start of a project.

through the hard labor required and take greater pride
and satisfaction in a job well done.

Experiencing multiple dimensions

As I professional writer, I have to address a wide
array of topics, often starting off knowing little or
nothing about them. But this intrigues me, I guess
because I find that virtually all things in life are
interesting. Several times, however, my confidence
has been shaken.

Once, for example, I received an assignment to
write speeches for the regional president of a multinational aluminum company. I was uncertain about
their environmental policies regarding a proposed
second dam on a scenic river where they generated hydroelectricity to power a giant smelter. So I
felt uncomfortable taking on the project and lacked
confidence that, if I did, I would be able to produce
a quality product.

I decided to travel to the north to look at the
company's operations for myself. I was astonished
by what I saw. Taking industrial tours has always intrigued me, for it allows me to experience firsthand
aspects of life far removed from my own day-to-day
world. The company's existing smelter used older
technology and appeared like a scene from Dante's
Inferno. Flames leapt from gigantic furnaces, red
molten aluminum seeped along tracks in the floor
like lava, and smoke billowed through cavernous
work halls. It felt overwhelming and alien.

And yet, I contemplated, how much we all use
things made of aluminum. Every day we buy and
use aluminum-based products – from canned drinks

to the laptop computer I'm typing on right now. We're all part of the consuming world even if at an idealistic level we oppose certain industries or developments. None of us is pure. (How many strict vegetarians do you know, for example, who never wear leather shoes or belts? Or political ideologues who absolutely never vary from their personal interpretation of "politically correct" in order to take advantage of some opportunity?)

The point is not to deaden your personal sensitivities but to realize that we're not separate from the world around us. There's far more commonality in the human experience than difference. By tapping into this commonality we can communicate far more effectively.

We can also find points of connection that enable us to shift perceptions and beliefs more to our own. In the case of the aluminum plant and its new generating facility, I hope the slant I gave to the speeches I wrote injected greater force into the company's commitment to conduct its proposed development in an ecologically responsible manner.

Fortunately, most of my projects have been more compatible with my own convictions. Once, for example, I assisted in the creation of a world center for dialogue. *Dialogue* means meeting with people not to persuade them to go along with your own viewpoint but to find commonality and from there solve problems jointly and creatively. While developing the center's mission statement and operating philosophy, I consulted with all the key people working to create the new institution.

When I wrote the material, I drew my inspiration from the writings of a nuclear physicist who had analyzed dialogue from the perspective of quantum mechanics. He argued that, like subatomic particles which connect with one another though separated by vast distances, and which pass through otherwise impenetrable barriers, people are intrinsically and literally interconnected. The principles of dialogue are founded on physical reality, he claimed. Here was something I profoundly believed in myself. This conviction imbued what I wrote with a strong and clear spirit that helped to unite people in a shared sense of meaningful, practical purpose.

Identify with your work

So how do we establish personal connection and conviction in our work? More problematic, how do we find personal conviction in work we don't necessarily identify with or totally agree with – hardly an uncommon situation.

Much of the cynicism that typifies our world grows out of a malaise of dissatisfaction in work.

As I've alluded to earlier, in the modern world many people do not find much personal satisfaction in their work. They're working to live, to make a living, not because they love their work or because they grew up with it as a traditional family trade.

Much of the cynicism that typifies our world grows out of a malaise of dissatisfaction in work. People learn to block out their feelings and carry out their eight-hour shifts (far longer in some parts of the world) in a kind of grudging trance. How could this not affect performance? When you see shoddy workmanship or encounter poor service, you can be sure alienation and dissatisfaction are lurking behind the surface. How different it is when you encounter someone who clearly enjoys his or her work.

Satisfaction and enjoyment coexist with personal conviction. Your task in creating effective communication or carrying out any kind of undertaking is to find meaning and identification in your work, to find a purpose you can believe in.

Discover a purpose you believe in.

For myself, when I fail to do this, I fall asleep on the job – literally. Many times in the course of writing something where I've failed to establish a personal connection, my eyes droop more and more until I slip off into a half sleep, nodding awake and drifting off again. The shock of such disassociation ought itself be enough to wake me up. Alas, it doesn't always work.

Here are some suggestions on how to use your power of conviction even when it seems at first you have no connection.

Realize personal relevance

Begin by identifying and articulating the core meaning and significance of whatever topic it is you're currently dealing with. Forget, for the moment, your own perspectives and prejudices and consider solely what is the essential heart of the matter at hand. Once you have a good idea of this, ask yourself how you personally feel about the issue. Look into your own life experiences and consider how you relate to the subject.

Realize personal relevance even if slim or indirect.

Even if it's a subject you don't seem to have personal ties to, you can always find points of connection or relevance. Say you're called on to devise an advertising campaign for a brand of cat food. But you've never owned a cat before; in fact, you don't even particularly like cats. But think back to your childhood. What about that neighbor who had cats? How did you feel about them? They were a bit mysterious; you felt a little frightened of their independence and aloofness. But they were also majestic, moving like sleek dancers. (I'm drawing on a story from my own life, but you can get the point.)

Now you have the beginnings of rich source of personal references to draw on and stimulate your creative thinking. Even though you may not like cats – I've grown to like them myself – you can appreciate them, and from this base of appreciation you can derive motivation and ideas. *Draw on personal reference to find relevance.*

Here's another example from my experience. Earlier in the book I mentioned an incident when I came up with the idea of shifting a Medieval-themed restaurant to the Renaissance to better reflect the chain's more upscale market. Although the restaurant didn't cater to my particular taste in food, I nonetheless enjoyed elaborating the Renaissance theme, working with my team to research the era and propose various thematic elements that could be incorporated into interior design, menu descriptions, and even recipes. In other words, I drew on an interest in history to feed my inspiration.

Actually, we always do things from personal perspective even if we think we're being totally objective. The "you" is there regardless when you tackle any subject or project. You cannot separate yourself from the act of communicating.

This might seem to contradict my earlier argument that communication requires open hearing – hearing the other inseparable from yourself. That you're inseparable, however, doesn't mean you're not also present as an individual. You're there; but you're also part of the equation.

Conviction arises from the dynamic interplay between you and others, between you and the world.

The trick is to become aware of the equation and the relationship. Ask yourself how you fit in. Uncover principles, meanings, angles, even slim threads of connection. Bring these to a conscious level; harness their energy. As you do so you will find that you do have a relationship with the subject and personal feelings about it. Relationships emerge from real life.

Conviction arises from the dynamic interplay between you and others, between you and the world.

Instead of burying your personal feelings, try to find intersections of commonality between your own convictions and whatever issue you're dealing with. Maybe where you thought there was no connection you will begin to see a point of reference, and from that a conjunction of sensitivity and meaning from which to draw inspiration. In other words, don't just write about the proposed aluminum smelter (drawing further on my example from above): consider how aluminum fits into your own life. Or how you feel about cats.

Your outlook counts

If it happens, and it does from time to time, that you find no personal connection whatsoever with a project you must deal with, try at least to alter its slant, shifting it more to your own perspective. Yes, be a little subversive.

You have an opportunity to bring your own conviction
to the work, why not take it? Why not express your own
views, subtly if necessary but using the leverage of your
position to influence a project's direction? Remember,
you're part of the equation.

Some might argue that finding personal connections
to something you inherently disagree with is an act of
hypocrisy. Occasionally that might be true, and I recommend that if you find yourself utterly, irretrievably
opposed in conscience to something you must write, say,
or do, get away from it. Withdraw diplomatically from
the task or, in an extreme case, resign from the post. Just
like soldiers pressed into committing illegal acts, you
should stand up and oppose what is inescapably wrong –
or somehow escape the situation altogether.

Shift things to your own view if need be.

*At every point in your life you have
the opportunity to find conviction in
your work and bring meaning to life.*

Given a truly open mind, however, you will rarely find
yourself in such extreme predicaments. Instead, you will
see points of intersection where you do relate to your
work. These relationships offer mines of opportunity for
creativity and communication. And when you find yourself stuck, facing a blank page, a poor first draft, or a confusing assignment of any kind, go back and reconnect.

At every point in your life you have the opportunity to
find conviction in your work and bring meaning to life.
In the very act of being attentive and caring, you form relationship. In communicating and acting from your own

truth, you create greater commonality with your fellow beings.

YOUR STORY

Are you facing a tough situation at work or elsewhere where you must deal with something you don't feel comfortable with or don't believe in? Describe the situation briefly and then list three to five aspects you relate to positively or negatively, or both. Now in one or two sentences, describe how you could go about turning the situation to something you can believe in and work with. Send your list and thoughts, anonymously if you wish, to www.WordsBecomeYou.com.

9

Write with Your Ears

Hear the voice inside you and realize how others perceive your words. Without compromising your own conviction, empathize with your audience and make your own points more telling.

EVERYTHING YOU WRITE OR EXPRESS, unless hidden away like a private diary, is heard, perceived, and interpreted by minds other than your own. Therefore, if you want to communicate effectively, cultivate your inherent sensitivity to how others hear you: hear with their ears. Empathize with your audience.

One way to do this is to nurture your aural sense for language – your innate inner ear. While writing something, actually hear your words as if you yourself were the reader or listener. The challenge is to do this without becoming excessively self-conscious and without compromising your own position and conviction.

MY STORY

Publicly speaking

Early in my career, I got a big break when I received a contract to create and then run the communications program in a newly established provincial department of consumer affairs. Barely in my mid-twenties, I found myself directing a staff of nearly thirty people and managing a huge budget to publicize new legislation, programs, and services for businesses and consumers.

Eighteen months later, I was given a temporary appointment to assist a special cabinet committee that was negotiating an agreement with the federal government on controlling then-rampant inflation. Suddenly I was cast onto a higher stage, meeting with top officials from across the country. I felt way in over my head.

Since I was a writer, I was called on one day to prepare a speech the provincial premier would deliver on the issue of inflation. I'd never written a speech before, and I can still remember the panic I felt worrying if I could do it. As I began to compose, I heard the words silently as if spoken inside my head. This led me to phrase the writing differently from a piece that would only be read, not read aloud. Speeches, as I began to appreciate, require a different kind voice and rhythm than printed communication.

But printed communication also has an aural dimension, and over time I began to pay greater attention to the voice inside my head that heard what I was writing and how others would hear it. I learned to write with my ears.

Knowing how others feel and perceive is a precious natural resource: it's the power of empathy. Some people find it easier to empathize with someone else than to express themselves; for others it's the reverse. The challenge for all of us is to do both – to feel empathy and express ourselves, the two forces working together as one.

Language arises from speech

The idea of speed-reading appealed to me as a young boy. I dreamed of using Superman-like powers to absorb vast amounts of literature in only hours or days. I would often look at the shiny new edition of the *Encyclopedia Britannica* that sat in a special bookcase in our home and imagine myself reading and memorizing it all. Of course, in those days I also fantasized that I was immortal and that my family would join me in living forever.

Along with that fantasy, the dream of speed-reading faded away. As my understanding of life grew more realistic, I also came to enjoy reading books slowly, almost mouthing the words, savoring the experience of steeping myself in an author's imaginary world or account of other lands, times, and lives than my own. I grew to love words, both spoken and written, so why speed through them, I concluded.

While writing something, actually hear your words as if you yourself were the reader or listener.

A relatively recent invention in the scheme of human existence, written language evolved over the past several thousand years, in contrast to many scores of thousands of years when people communicated through the spoken word and sign language. Hunters scouting the plains and the first plowers of fields exchanged information not with written notes but by speaking and signaling to one another. Even in more recent millennia, when the written language began to emerge, storytellers recorded history and myth, passing their community's legends down from generation to generation by word of mouth.

Although written language pervades our world today, live speech continues to hold sway. We go to films, watch television, plug music players into our ears, speak on the telephone, attend meetings, and chat with friends. Even electronic communication is transforming back to the spoken word with the advent of voice-over-Internet, built-in computer microphones, and voice-recognition programs.

Nevertheless, I remain fascinated by the written language and its history. Learning the derivation of words has always intrigued me. I'm convinced that even in a modern context the ancient root meanings of words affect the impressions we receive when we read. The past is present.

Language originated from speech, and sounds still pervade the written form. Even when we read, at some level of our consciousness we hear.

Recently, I've begun to study Chinese characters and enjoyed exploring a different dimension in written expression. Chinese characters convey meaning largely through vestiges of literal and symbolic imagery. A Chinese scholar once told me that a fluent reader of Chinese experiences reading more like watching a film of passing images rather than recognizing sequences of letters, as we do when reading English or other alphabetic languages. The two radically different types of writing, he said, use different sides of the brain.

Our alphabet also originated from pictures, some 3500 to 4000 years ago according to the latest evidence. The letter *M* or *m,* for example, had earlier stood on its own to mean the sea, its swoops portraying ocean waves. Similarly, the letter *A,* which originally sat on its side, had pictured an ox head. At some point in early Semitic and Phoenician history, a genius, or more likely a collective culture of genius, transformed the symbols so that in future each would stand for the first sound of its prior meaning. The word for sea, for example, presumably sounded like *em;* so in future *m,* the symbol for sea, would stand for the *em* sound in any word.

This revolutionary principle enabled people to use relatively few symbols, twenty-six in the case of English, to write thousands of words. By comparison, written Chinese is far more complicated to learn, requiring a knowledge of roughly 5000 characters to be fully literate. Each word consists of a unique character or combination of two, although the characters themselves are made up of a far smaller number of common elements. It's not that alphabetic languages are superior, however; they're just different.

Regardless, all languages (other than sign language, another marvelous system of communication) share a common trait − speech. Language is fundamentally a spoken medium. Language originated from speech, and sounds still pervade the written form. Even when we read, at some level of our consciousness we hear. Something inside our heads, if not the mouth itself, is mouthing what our eyes are seeing.

Hearing sharpens clarity

Teachers often advise students to read their drafts aloud to themselves in order to find errors in grammar, syntax, spelling, and punctuation. Taking the time to read aloud and listen can reveal mistakes that you otherwise may *Read drafts* miss when you review your drafts silently. As you visually *aloud to spot* read and reread what you've composed in written form, *errors missed* you unconsciously skip over many words and phrases, fo- *in reading* cusing instead on the flow of the writing and thus missing *silently.* mistakes. Reading aloud compensates for this.

Hearing your writing spoken also makes sloppy or short-circuited thinking more apparent. It's as if to some degree, after having silently read your own writing many times, you're reading partly from memory rather than see-ing exactly what's on the page. Reading aloud forces you to slow down and go over everything in greater detail.

From a young age, especially if we read a lot, we develop an inner ear for our language's standard usage.

An even more effective method for editing your writ-ing is to enlist someone who hasn't seen it before to read it aloud. While that person may spot spelling and *Enlist others to* punctuation errors that you in your familiarity with the *read your work* writing no longer see, you're able to hear the sense and *to you.* flow of your language spoken freshly in someone else's voice. If, as the old saying goes, "Seeing is believing," hearing is revealing.

Note, though, that silent reading also helps when re-viewing your drafts. Our ear tolerates greater flexibility

with grammar and syntax. So don't expect to catch all of
your errors when you hear your draft read aloud, whereas
your eyes will almost instinctively react when you read
incorrect grammar or syntax. From a young age, especially if we read a lot, we develop an inner ear for our
language's standard usage. But the inner ear's aptitude can
provide even more service.

Balancing belief and critique

Through many years of writing professionally, I've developed a knack for subtly hearing what my writing sounds
like at the same time as I'm engaged in composing it. A
little editor is functioning inside my head. Like a sixth
sense, my inner ear operates automatically, listening in to
everything I write and checking to make sure that others
will comprehend it as I intend.

Everyone has the capacity to use this deeper form of
hearing; I've merely cultivated it as part of my work.
You're already hearing with your inner ear, but you're
likely not fully aware of it or you haven't come to trust
it and learned to use it confidently. Writing with your
ears requires a bit of attention and practice. But you can
do it.

"Hear" your
writing while
composing it.

In tapping this ability, however, find a balance between
conviction and self-critique. Appreciate how others hear
your words, but what you say and write should be driven
by what you believe. Don't let your inner editor censor
self-expression. Empathy means feeling how others feel;
it doesn't mean denying yourself.

So write fearlessly, not doubting what you have to say
or your ability to say it. Let your expression flow freely.
Particularly when reviewing and revising your work,
however, don't be so consumed by your conviction that
you fail to realize when your writing makes no sense to

your readers or alienates them so much that they won't hear you. In other words, act confidently while also heedful of the impressions you leave.

But how can you act heedfully and yet with personal conviction at the same time? These two activities seem contradictory. How can you do two apparently opposite things — expressing and hearing — simultaneously? Opposites cancel each other out. Right?

Somehow we humans think we have to have everything all black or all white. We need to believe that we're right and others are wrong. The answer must always be yes or no. Others are our enemy or our friend. My belief system is true; others, false.

Reality is different. Most things are both right and wrong, this and that, at the same time. Nothing is perfectly black or white, but rather somewhere on a scale between the two — actually oscillating between the two. We are at the same time a unique individual and a part of society. We are citizens of our own nation but also of the world. People hold to different values, customs, and beliefs, but all the world's people exist on one planet, in one universe.

Don't get stuck in seeing just "this or that."

These apparent contradictions portray the natural order of things. Tapping into your distinctiveness as well as your commonality with others gives you the power and energy to live and create as an individual but also in harmony with the world. The world is out of harmony and troubles arise between individuals and among nations because people get stuck in believing one side of the equation only: that they alone are right; that everything is black or everything is white.

The interplay between distinctiveness and complexity plays out at the level of communication, where you can express yourself based on your own truth and yet also remain sensitive and connected to your fellow beings, to your listeners and readers, and to their truths. The key to achieving a balance between expression and impression is to realize, once again, that change is the only constant. If you become fixated on your own convictions and perceptions, believing they are permanent and inviolable and that they form your identity alone, then your mind closes. You hear only yourself.

When you keep an open mind, responding to life's ever-unfolding and ever-changing reality, you can do two things at once: you can be yourself and you can connect with others. And that's communication.

Free of a fixed idea of yourself, you can hear what you're writing or saying, feeling its sensibility and impact on others, while also allowing your creative juices to flow unimpeded. The closer these two seemingly contrary but, in fact, compatible mind-sets – self and other – come together, come into balance, the more cogent and effective your communication will be.

When you keep an open mind, responding to life's ever-unfolding and ever-changing reality, you can do two things at once: you can be yourself and you can connect with others. And that's communication.

YOUR STORY

Write a paragraph about an issue you're currently facing at work or home. Read it silently to yourself. Try at the same time to hear how the words will come across to others. Try the same exercise reading your paragraph aloud. Now, rewrite your original paragraph reflecting any insights you gained? Submit the two paragraphs plus a brief list of any particular observations to www.WordsBecomeYou.com. Then share the website with friends and coworkers.

10

Trust Yourself

Living naturally and fluidly, open and responsive to the world around you, you gain confidence and peace of mind in continuously experiencing, creating, connecting – and living. Trust yourself and words become you.

SURPRISING THOUGH IT MAY SEEM, I hope that by now you've found this book a little repetitive. Not boring, I hope, but yes, repetitive. Not incidentally, each chapter echoes the others. Each chapter expresses the power of confidence from a different perspective.

Recapping, the book began by encouraging you to trust your inborn *insight* to come up with ideas from "nothing" and "nowhere." Count on your natural ability for *perception* to understand the world around you. Rely on your gut *intuition* and respond to the subtle signs you feel. Trust your aptitude for handling complexity with simplicity through the power of *synthesis*. And cultivate *creativity* by boldly reinventing ways of doing things rather than depending on what you and others have done before. Yes, do reinvent the wheel.

The book then described specific techniques for achieving *clarity* by exploiting your instinctive facility to bring order out of chaos and organize even the most complex material. The next three chapters urged you to *articulate* your main idea fearlessly at the start; to speak your own truth with *conviction;* but also to hear your inner ear, appreciating with *empathy* how others perceive what you write or say.

These nine faculties all boil down to one final, tenth power: trusting yourself – *confidence* – the subject of this concluding chapter.

People often talk about self-confidence. But exactly what *self* are they talking about? What self am I talking about? What is the self you should trust?

Fearing nothing

Deep down, most of us in some way are a bit terrified of ourselves. During our childhood and education and throughout our working and social lives, we've learned to control our behavior, actions, emotions, and words. Another little voice inside warns us that, if we don't control ourselves, we might do bad things, make serious mistakes, hurt others, or get hurt ourselves. If we speak our mind and act forthrightly, we might undermine our livelihood, our family's well-being, and our very survival.

Of course, I'm reflecting on the person I've come to know best – my own nature. But I know that virtually all individuals and families and all groups and nations express self-doubt in one way or another. Lack of confidence and its distortion of behavior are a universal human experience. Insecurity manifests as fear, hesitation, deceit, anger, prejudice, greed, violence, and a myriad of other neuroses and sociopathic behaviors.

Stop doubting yourself.

The doubting self-editor is busy at work throughout our waking lives, often operating just barely below or above the conscious level, sometimes emerging full blown, terrifying us and leading us to doubt everything.

This self-editor is not the "hearing ear" discussed in the last chapter, which simply realizes how others perceive our words. The self-editor addressed here is a frightened little self.

And this little, frightened self asks itself, "If I let myself simply be – just doing things instinctively without first thinking them through – won't I act a little crazy? Maybe if I really let loose, I'll turn into something evil and nasty, a mini-Hitler or mini-Stalin, forcing my will on others? Better that I suppress my wild side, controlling what I do and say." Or some other variation of self-doubt and self-deprecation. Or the flip side: feeling superior and pushing everyone out of my way to get what I alone want. This sort of self-centered dysfunction typifies whole nations as well as individuals and actually derives from insecurity not strength.

This little, frightened self – the mind that keeps jabbering away all the time in the background – is not the self I'm advising you to trust. I don't believe that monsters like Hitler, Stalin, Pol Pot, or Idi Amin actually trusted themselves. Their behavior wasn't free and uninhibited. They and other truly evil people are at heart deeply repressed. Their actions aren't natural; they're corrupted by hideous fears. The little voices inside that whisper self-doubt to all of us scream at them, deafening their sensitivity to others and driving them to madness. Such people are bullies of the worst sort, acting out in horrible ways to cover deep-set, often unconscious but insidious, fears and self-doubts.

Human beings are born without the doubting self. Babies instinctively connect with everyone and everything in their immediate world. They aren't lying there on their backs or crawling around on the floor worried about how they look or how they'll be judged. They're simply exploring, hungry, tired, burping, defecating, smiling, crying, and responding spontaneously to their world. We retain this natural connection but, unfortunately, it gets compromised and often twisted by the influences that hurt us, tell us we're bad, or otherwise repress our natural instincts.

Fortunately we can draw on all sorts of ways to renew and revitalize our inborn, wholesome self. Straightforward work like gardening, cleaning house, cooking, or carpentry can help. Meditation techniques of various sorts prove effective for some people. Others find that rigorous exercise – walking, running, swimming, biking, and so forth – acts like meditation and quiets the little, terrified self editor.

Most of the time, you don't have to think what words to speak; they arise spontaneously, virtually instinctively – hence, fluently.

Essentially, it takes practice, a lifetime of practice to simply be and trust ourselves. Perhaps it is our life practice. Perhaps it's our purpose in life: to evolve with growing self-confidence, at peace with ourselves and living actively in greater harmony with the world.

Being and evolving

One of the most effective ways to evolve as a human being is to continually deepen your communication. Learn to trust yourself – to find yourself – by finding confidence in your inherent ability to connect with your fellow human beings.

Just to give one example, when you begin writing something, after all of your research, outlining, and thought, put aside your plans and notes – and doubts – and allow yourself to write freely and directly. Turn off the little doubting, negative editor inside. Don't worry about mistakes, contradictions, or awkwardness. Everything can be checked, corrected, and edited later.

Writing is like speaking your native language: most of the time, you don't have to think what words to speak; they arise spontaneously, virtually instinctively – hence, fluently. Writing can work the same way. Let it flow. Trust yourself.

If you get stuck, don't worry. As I've advised earlier, just skip the sentence, paragraph, or section you're stuck in and go on to the next. You can always come back and fill in any gaps. Having a few gaps to fill is less intimidating than facing an entirely empty document. How to fill the gaps becomes clearer and easier when you've completed the surrounding material.

Skipping problems and returning to them later is a variation on the knack of giving yourself a break, pausing and turning your mind to other things rather than pounding your head against the wall trying to figure something out. We all have a tendency to be far too hard on ourselves. If we each took life easier, life would be easier for all of us.

Gaining confidence entails learning how not to be stuck – stuck in habits from the past, stuck in narrow thinking, bogged down in fears of the unknown. The secret to practicing being yourself and not being stuck is to live a full life, responsive to the world around you and to other people, as they actually are, now, moment by moment.

Margin notes:

Put aside your notes and worries and write freely.

Skip over problems and return to them later.

Self and other

Most of us assume that to learn or write about something we must focus our attention on that subject alone. But, as I've suggested earlier in the book, inquiry and communication also require living a full life, gaining knowledge from beyond our usual patterns of thinking and experience: in other words, realizing that everything in life is interesting and related. The more we experience and absorb, the more we gain power to handle the endless challenges we encounter.

At first this may seem contradictory: that to address specific issues you must cultivate an expansive knowledge. Experiencing life deeply and broadly, however, makes you more open and receptive and able to communicate effectively. Openness cultivates your natural wisdom – your inherent ability to perceive, understand, and connect.

Discover your natural wisdom.

Narrow experience and narrow thinking debilitate life. Life forms of any kind grow weak and vulnerable when they inbreed too much and become overly specialized. For example, highly "advanced" or genetically modified varieties of corn while perhaps bountiful are also far more vulnerable to disease. Hardy original varieties are often tougher.

Variety and exchange make for healthier living. The most successful and creative societies are those most open to other cultures and diversity of thinking. The European Renaissance, for example, was nurtured by the rediscovery of ancient Greek and Roman texts that had been preserved by the Arab civilization.

The ancient Chinese Tang Dynasty capital of Chang'an was perhaps the grandest and most cosmopolitan city of its time, with people from other parts of the world contributing to its wealth of culture and technology. The United States, Canada, and Australia are three countries whose vitality has been fed by high rates of immigration. In our own era, the advanced technology and digital revolution were born in regions with diverse educational institutions and open-minded thinking.

Our minds and communication skills function in the same fashion. Diversity of experience and knowledge cultivates our ability to cope and get in touch. We discover and express ideas not merely by devising logical and linear sequences of words or images, but by recombining elements drawn from the whole universe of our minds. The bigger the universe we experience – both in breadth and depth – the bigger our minds.

Embrace change and diversity.

The most successful and creative societies are those most open to other cultures and diversity of thinking.

Too many people and too many groups feel threatened by diversity. They see others as a threat. But a threat to what? A threat to their singular identity. So much of our identity is wrapped up in a fixed, set concept of ourselves. We think we're unchanging and permanent. This is denial. Everything in life changes, nothing is permanent.

People and societies who are more confident in themselves – a self that is fluid, experiences life fully, and lives dynamically – are not threatened by otherness. Alive in their security they communicate with greater confidence and openness. What an irony that to relate effectively, sensitive to others, you must act out of greater confidence in your own identity: an identity that is not fixed and immutable but forever flowing and changing.

Let words become you

Like ideas and insights that arise from nothing, the self itself arises from nothing – but a nothing that is devoid only of a narrow, fixed idea of self. As described in the first chapter, this nothing is part of everything, teeming with life. It's the center of your being. Live from the center of your being in this ever-changing reality and discover that communication is natural. Communication is your birthright.

Acting naturally, fluently, and responsively you will find confidence and peace of mind in continuously experiencing, creating, connecting – and living. Be confident in continually reinventing everything in your world, including yourself. You're already in touch.

Take it easy – you're already in touch.

Be confident in continually reinventing everything in your world, including yourself.

Early in the book, I noted that most of us feel stressed by even the thought of writing something or speaking to an audience. Stress easily turns to fear. I remember as a child, a few years after the end of World War II, watching film clips showing Franklin D. Roosevelt giving a radio address in which he emboldened the American people on the eve of the country's entering the war by saying, "There is nothing to fear but fear itself."

I would take this counsel a step further and say, "Do not fear even fear itself." From time to time and, for some people, a great deal of the time, we experience fear – and anger, hatred, judgmentalism, jealousy, greed, and

the other ills that haunt us. If we worry about fear itself,
however, or try to cover it up, it just buries itself deeper,
tightening its grip on us. If instead we acknowledge it to
ourselves, fear gradually releases its hold over us, freeing
more and more of our potential as human beings, the potential we were born with, the potential to connect with
others, to communicate, and to live in greater harmony.
Trust yourself and words that fit you come naturally –
words become you.

This book

My story is this book, so for this chapter I've put my
personal story last. When I started writing the book,
I was worried that I didn't have enough to say or
anything substantial enough to interest people. But
then I realized what I have to say is, indeed, quite
simple. Life itself is simple; we complicate things far
too much, making things bigger and more complex
than they are in reality.

So I grew confident that, as described in the
fourth chapter, I had synthesized all of my thinking about writing and communication down to
one guiding concept – self-confidence – thus gaining perspective for myself and the ability to share it
with my audience. This single idea is not a false one,
for with conviction I'm speaking my truth.

I feel no fear that so many experts have already
written about communication. The ideas and suggestions I set out in this book no doubt have already
appeared, perhaps in some other form, in other
books. I don't know; I didn't look. I didn't consult
other books on communication before writing my
own. I'm comfortable reinventing the wheel.

Moreover, as my old history professor used to say, "Nothing new since Plato." By this he meant that all the ideas that shaped Western civilization had already been formulated by the time of the Ancient Greeks. Knowing that human experience is a constant, however, doesn't bind our imagination; it empowers us to continually live freshly in the ever-changing now.

As I developed this book and elaborated my central theme, I went through a lengthy iterative process of figuring out what techniques have worked successfully for me over the past twenty years of writing and consulting on communication. In other words, I found clarity for my ideas, expressing them in the ten chapters that make up this book, bringing order out of chaos.

For a long time, I was stumped to come up with a title. Oh, I thought of plenty of good titles; but every one had already been used. (In this case, I did look at other books.) Sometimes I felt frustrated; that's only natural. But I trusted that eventually an original title – more importantly, a suitable one – would emerge. After all, that's what this chapter, and really the entire book, is about: trusting one's self. And finally, just after finishing a later draft, a suitable title did emerge – suddenly, from nothing. The words became me.

In a deeper sense, the doing of this book is more vital for me personally than the words or ideas themselves. Actions are more important than words. How we actively relate to other people and the world we're part of defines us far more than what we say or think, preach or pray. So, in truth, I've done this book not for me but for you.

One final word: Never forget that words can lie. Way too often we let false words, those of others and our own, shape our sense of self. Negative self-images; delusions of wealth and power; bigotries fostered by ideologues; propaganda of any stripe or sort, political or commercial – if believed, these deceptions fixate our identity, weaken our powers, and loosen our bonds to our fellow beings and the world that is our home. *Words* have then become us in the worst sense, pigeonholing us and narrowing our sense of identity; or the reverse, when we use words to stereotype and belittle others.

These are not the becoming words Duncan spoke of to his loyal captain, quoted at the beginning of this book from Shakespeare's *Macbeth*. The captain's words were as true as his bleeding wounds. Thus Duncan said, "Thy words become thee." True words are those that suit you. These are the words that best *become you*.

As I suggested in the introduction, you don't really need this book. It merely helps you gain insight on how to liberate and use the powers you already have. So throw the book away (figuratively speaking). Trust yourself, and words become you. You become you.

YOUR STORY

Has this book shed light on your own life or helped you gain greater confidence in your own potential? Compose a list of three to five additional powers of communication which you think we inherently possess as human beings. Send your personal list to www.WordsBecomeYou.com. And if you found *Words Become You* insightful or useful in any way, let the word out: tell friends, family, and coworkers about it.

Acknowledgments

Many people have contributed to my understanding of communication – and life. First, I want to acknowledge the writers, editors, graphic designers, printers, and other communication practitioners who have been my friends and colleagues over the years, including Don Atkins, Tim Carter, Maya Grip, Joseph Heald, Hal Holden, Barbara Tomlin, Claudette Reed Upton, and the late Marilyn Sacks; with special appreciation to Frank Anfield, Rick Archbold, Roberto Dosil, Mike Savage, Kosta Tsetsekas, and most of all Ben Ze Wang for their help and advice on this book. Next, thank you to my editor, Ruth Wilson, and to Kathy Kimball for her thoughtful review. As well, I wish to express my appreciation to the clients I've had over the years who have encouraged and supported my thinking and creativity: Jack Blaney, Gordon Diamond, Robert Fouquet, William A.W. Neilson, the late Louise Spratley, and the late Neil Weatherston. Finally, a special thank you to my longtime friends Alistair MacKay, Albarosa Simonetti, Steven Lemay, Marta Farevaag, and Andreas Naumann, who all encouraged me to write this book; to my late brother, Ken, a great scholar and educator whose values like my own came from our parents; and to Eshin John Godfrey, friend and teacher.

Index